LRTA REGIONAL HAND
No 1

TRAMWAYS OF THE
EAST MIDLANDS

by R.J.S. Wiseman

based on the original work by
W.H.Bett & J.C. Gillham

LRTA

Previous Page
Leicester Corporation No. 42 at the city terminus in Bowling Green Street awaits departure to Aylestone on 26 May 1938. *(W.A.Camwell National Tramway Museum*

Above
An Ilkeston Corporation car at Ilkeston Market Place in May 1903. *(R.B.Parr National Tramway Museum*

Front Cover
Market Street, Nottingham viewed from the Market Place circa 1907 showing a tram for Bulwell. New trams now use double track in Market Street on their journey to Bulwell and Hucknell. *(Painting by Ashley Best*

Back Cover
The Incentro trams of Nottingham Express Transit run in all weather conditions. In the upper view No 208 is seen ascending from the Forest stop up snow covered Mount Hooton Road while below No. 203 descends Waverley Street on a wet afternoon overshadowed by the trees of the arboretum. 15 October 2004.
(Steven Dee, R.J.S.Wiseman

Published by Light Rail Transit Association
7 Ramsdale Court, Scarborough, YO11 2AP

ISBN
978-0-948106-35-4

Designed by Just My Type, Isle of Wight PO37 6EA
Printed by Delmar Press Ltd, Nantwich, Cheshire CW5 5LS

TRAMWAYS OF THE EAST MIDLANDS

Introduction

The series of regional handbooks has a history going back to articles published in The Modern Tramway during the years 1938-39. Under the title "Great British Tramway Networks" the late Wingate.H.Bett wrote ten articles starting in May 1938 with North Midlands and concluding in June 1939 with West Midlands. An eleventh article by John.C.Gillham completed the series in August 1939. These articles proved popular and were incorporated into an 88-page book under the same title, by Wingate H.Bett and J.C.Gillham, in 1940. It included East Scotland and South Wales which had not been published in *The Modern Tramway.*

The book was sold out by the end of 1943 and a second edition of 96 pages was published in 1944. This lasted until 1957 when a greatly enlarged third edition of 224 pages was published with a fourth edition of 200 pages in 1962 under the same joint authorship.

When supplies of this last edition were exhausted it was decided not to reprint the work but to publish a series of regional handbooks under the editorship of the late J.H.Price. The first was the North Midlands published at 40p in 1974, others followed in succession: South Yorkshire & Humberside in 1975, South East Lancashire in 1976, North East England in 1977, East Anglia in 1981, North Lancashire in 1985, South West England in 1990, South Midlands and Kent,the latter by G.E.Baddeley, in 1992, and South Wales in 1994. Later volumes were West Midlands, edited by R.J.S. Wiseman, followed by West Yorkshire, East Scotland, West Scotland, South Lancashire and North Wales, and finally Tramways of the South Coast; the later volumes by J.C.Gillham and R.J.S.Wiseman.

An enlarged edition of the North Midlands book, more correctly entitled *Tramways of the East Midlands*, was published in 1979 with extra pages. This edition is now almost out of print and the opportunity has been taken to publish a new edition under the above title.

There are four cities within the East Midlands area, Derby, Nottingham, Leicester and Lincoln. Each had a municipal tramway system and it was proposed to link Derby and Nottingham.

In this volume we start our tour in the north at Chesterfield and follow the line of the Midland Railway through to Burton-upon-Trent, visiting Crich, Matlock and Derby en-route. Returning to Chesterfield, we then follow the line of the Great Central Railway through Mansfield to Nottingham, then out to Ripley and Ilkeston before returning to Nottingham and continuing to Loughborough and Leicester. Finally we visit Lincoln and the Alford and Sutton tramway.

Editor's note

To be asked to step into shoes previously occupied by Richard Wiseman, John Price and the Wingate Bett/John Gillham partnership is a daunting honour, though my appointment as series editor for a new run of LRTA Regional Handbooks is not a solitary task, since other experts will be helping me on a volume by volume basis. Of course most of the detailed research was carried out by those previous editors, so my task should not be equated with theirs. Rather I hope to move publications along rather more quickly, aided by the production facilities of Just My Type with my wife, Janet Taplin, at the keyboard. She is well-experienced in LRTA book production, with Freiburg, Innsbruck, Halifax, Vicinal and most recently Rochdale bearing her imprint.

Although officially 'retired', Richard Wiseman had much of East Midlands already done, so here my task has required an even lighter touch; thank you Richard for your efforts. The cartography is by Roger Smith, whose clear and detailed maps have graced these volumes for several years, and I am grateful for his dedicated work.

Michael Taplin
Shanklin, September 2007

Chesterfield

Chesterfield is an ancient borough and market centre in north east Derbyshire on the River Rother some twelve miles to the south of Sheffield on the northern flank of the large Derbyshire, Nottinghamshire coalfield. To the west lies agricultural land and easy access to the Derbyshire Dales. The crooked spire of the church of St.Mary and All Saints dominates the scene.

The Chesterfield and District Tramways Company obtained an Act in 1879 to build a tramway, 4 miles long from Brampton through the town centre to Whittington, but only the section to Brampton, 2 miles, was built. It was opened on 8 November 1882 and worked by three Ashbury-built tramcars. The Company was not successful and was succeeded by the Chesterfield Tramways Company in December 1886. The new company purchased two further cars and continued operation until the tramway passed to the Corporation on 22 November 1897. The Corporation took some time before obtaining an Act for an electric tramway and the horse trams continued in operation until late in 1904.

Another tramway scheme that did not come to fruition was the Chesterfield, Hasland and North Wingfield Tramways. This line of seven miles would have served a number of colliery villages to the south-east of the town, but the Bill was unexpectedly withdrawn in August 1887.

The Corporation opened the electric tramway from the town centre to Brampton on 23 December 1904 without ceremony. On Christmas Eve the service was extended northwards to the borough boundary at Stonegravels. The final section through the Newbold and Dunston area to Whittington Moor opened on 31 January 1905.

Although a deputation from the Hasland Parish Council tried to persuade Chesterfield in 1906 to build the Hasland line, this was never done, nor was the branch south along the Derby Road as far as Birdholme.

The tramway was served by 18 or possibly 19 Brush-built open-top and balcony cars of which No.7, now at the National Tramway Museum at Crich is still extant. The tracks were well beyond their sell-by date when the last tram, No.14, ran on 23 May 1927. The replacing trolley-buses were, in their turn, replaced by motor buses in 1938.

Chesterfield horse car No.1 at the Low Pavement terminus. Nos. 1 and 2 were of Eade's reversible type with only one staircase.   *(Courtesy of National Tramway Museum*

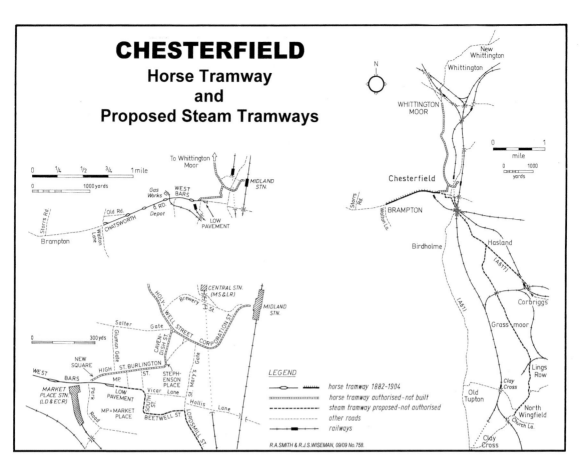

CHESTERFIELD
Horse Tramway
and
Proposed Steam Tramways

LEGEND

○—⊕——◼◼◼◼	horse tramway 1882-1904
▭▭▭▭▭▭	horse tramway authorised-not built
- - - - - -	steam tramway proposed-not authorised
· · · · · ·	other roads
+—◼—+	railways

R.A.SMITH & R.J.S.WISEMAN, 09/09 No.758.

One of the 1914 Brush cars, probably No.18. at Whittington Moor terminus. The authorised tramway along the Sheffield Road to the left, as far as St. John's Road was not built.

(Commercial card, courtesy National Tramway Museum

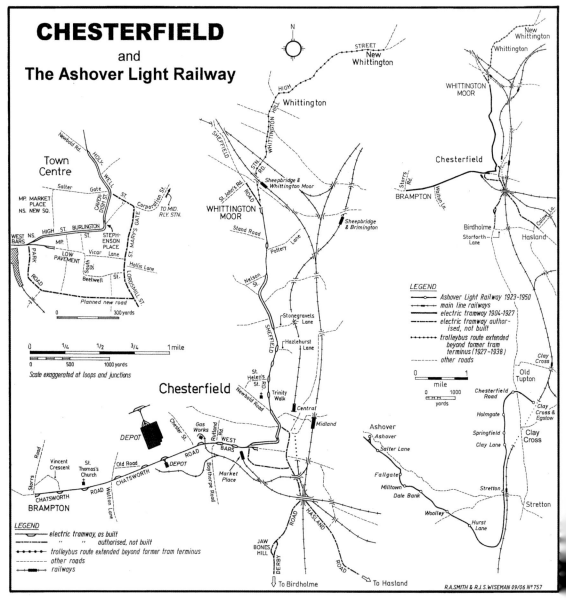

CHESTERFIELD
and
The Ashover Light Railway

Town Centre

LEGEND
— electric tramway, as built
" " " authorised, not built
••••• trolleybus route extended beyond former tram terminus
---- other roads
+-+-+ railways

LEGEND
—○— Ashover Light Railway 1923–1950
-+-+- main line railways
——— electric tramway 1904–1927
-·-·- electric tramway authorised, not built
•••••• trolleybus route extended beyond former tram terminus (1927–1938)
---- other roads

Scale exaggerated at loops and junctions

R.A.SMITH & R.J.S.WISEMAN 09/06 N° 757

No. 7 `now in the Crich collection, at Stephenson Place. As the conductor is turning the trolley the photograph was probably taken on a Saturday when the through service was suspended.
(Commercial card, courtesy National Tramway Museum

Looking down from the High Street an unknown Chesterfield tram has just turned into Burlington Street on its way to Brampton. St Mary's Church with its famous crooked spire is very evident. The double tracks take up the whole of the street and it is just as well that there are few cars around in the nineteen twenties. *(Commercial card*

Although the passenger service on the Ashover Light Railway was withdrawn in 1936 a special train was arranged on 24 August 1947 for the Manchester Locomotive Society, The Birmingham Locomotive Club and the Midland area of the Stephenson Locomotive Society. Open wagons were used on this occasion; there were four coaches, two of which saw service on the Lincolnshire Coast Light Railway near Cleethorpes . (W.A.Camwell, courtesy National Tramway Museum

Clay Cross

Continuing south following the Midland Railway along the upper reaches of the Rother valley for five miles, we arrive at Clay Cross a small town which thanks to the driving force of George Stephenson developed coal mines and an iron works. The Clay Cross Company opened the 2ft.0in.gauge Ashover Light railway on 7 April 1925 to bring stone from quarries to the works. It followed the Midland Railway south to Stretton from where it followed the Amber valley north-west to Ashover. It was steam operated and ran a passenger service until 13 September 1936, summer only from 1931, with carriages built in tramway tradition with end balconies and wooden longitudinal seats. The line closed on 31 March 1950 and part now lies under Ogston reservoir. Proposals to re-open part of the line came to nought in the 1960's, but in 2006 the Ashover Light Railway Society was formed with the object of re-opening the line from Ogston Reservoir at Woolley northwards to Ashover.

Crich

The North Midland Railway was surveyed by George Stephenson and continued south from Clay Cross to Derby via Ambergate where he built a limeworks. The limestone came from his quarries at Crich two miles away. To convey the stone he opened in 1841 a metre gauge tramway which included an incline, worked by steam locomotives from 1897 and later diesel units. The Clay Cross Company closed the line in 1957 and part of the site was acquired by the Tramway Museum Society in 1959 as the site for its museum. The first tram, Cardiff Water Car No.131, arrived on 8 April of that year.

Almost a half-century later Crich Tramway Village has been developed with almost one mile of standard gauge track from Town End to Glory Mine. The Society has over sixty tramcars, both passenger and works, horse, steam and electric drawn from every part of the British Isles and overseas,either operational or on display in depots or in an exhibition hall. There is a library and reading room where research may take place together with other visitor attractions including shops, restaurant facilities at the Red Lion and a woodland walk. The museum is open daily from April to October and then at weekends until Christmas.

Leicester 76, rescued from a cricket ground at East Cowick, near Snaith, was among the fifteen trams that arrived at Crich during 1960. It was restored to operating condition by 1973 and ran for three years. It is seen newly restored in 1969. It is now in the exhibition hall. (R.J.S. Wiseman

No. 812 was the first of seven Glasgow passenger trams to arrive at Crich. It is seen here crossing the bridge over the old mineral railway at the site entrance on 13 August 1960. It was followed by No. 1068, now Paisley 68, three weeks later. *(R.J.S. Wiseman*

812 is taken into the site and then off loaded with a crane. Leeds 600 is in the background 13 August 1960. *(R.J.S. Wiseman*

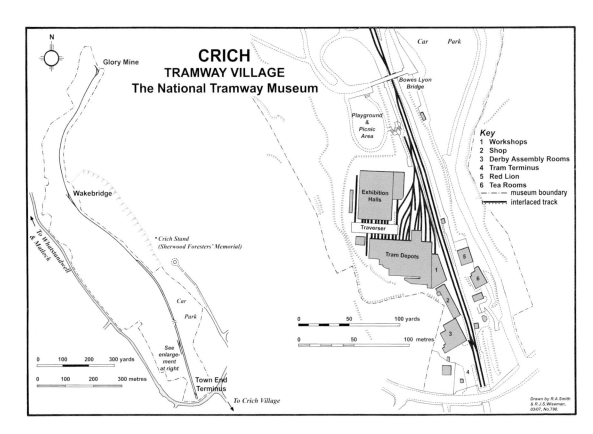

There are now five London trams at the Crich Museum. Four of them had arrived by 5 July 1997 when this view of LCC1, restored by the LCC Tramway Trust, was taken. Behind is Metropolitan 331 with LPTB 1622 in the background. (R.J.S. Wiseman

Matlock

The section of the Crich tramway high on the hillside from Wakebridge to Glory Mine offers fine views over the Derwent Valley to the west. If we descend to the valley at Cromford, one time terminus of the Cromford & High Peak Tramway, closed in 1967, we then follow the valley through Matlock Bath to Matlock, a popular inland holiday destination with many hotels. One of these was Smedley's Hydro about halfway up on Matlock Bank and to reach it and the higher parts of the town a cable tramway was proposed by local citizens including Sir George Newnes MP, the famous music publisher. The line, 0.62 miles long with a maximum gradient of 1 in 5, was opened with due ceremony on 28 March 1893 by the Matlock Cable Tramway Co.Ltd. The Company also proposed an electric tramway through to Matlock Bath but the old bridge over the Derwent was too weak for a tramway.

Sir George Newnes bought out the other shareholders and formally presented the tramway to the Matlock Council as a gift on 28 October 1898. The tramway was worked by three George F. Milnes double-deck open-top eight-wheel tramcars, with detachable grippers acting on an endless cable similar to the Edinburgh Northern Company. On 23 September 1927 the Council decided to close the tramway, the steepest street tramway in the world, but the cable broke a week later and was not replaced.

In 1904 there were proposals for an electric tramway from Rowsley through the Matlocks to Cromford, and in 1911 trolleybuses were proposed, but no progress was made. However in 1984 an aerial cableway, 568 metres long was built to serve the Heights of Abraham.

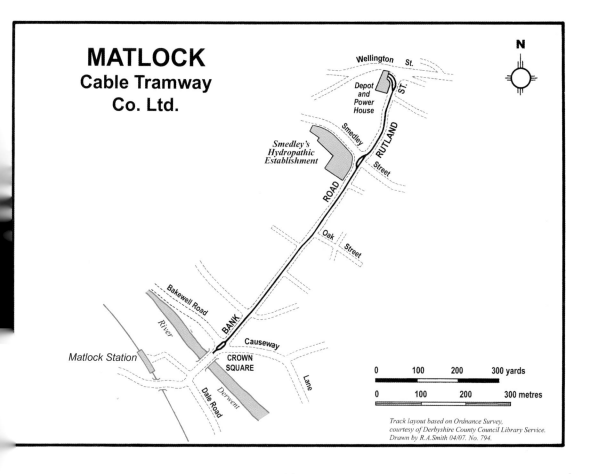

MATLOCK
Cable Tramway
Co. Ltd.

Wellington St.

Depot and Power House

RUTLAND ST

Smedley's Hydropathic Establishment

Smedley Street

ROAD

Oak Street

Bakewell Road

River

BANK

Causeway

Matlock Station

CROWN SQUARE

Lane

Dale Road

Derwent

N

| 0 | 100 | 200 | 300 yards |

| 0 | 100 | 200 | 300 metres |

Track layout based on Ordnance Survey, courtesy of Derbyshire County Council Library Service. Drawn by R.A.Smith 04/07. No. 794.

A view of No. 1 at Crown Square. The elaborate shelter was removed in 1927 to a nearby park and the leaded glass is now at the National Tramway Museum.
(F.T.W Dennis & Sons, courtesy National Tramway Museum.

Nos. 2 and 3 at the Halfway at Smedley Street. No. 3 will continue up Rutland Street to the terminus at Wellington Street.
(Courtesy National Tramway Museum.

No. 1 at Crown Square terminus. The steepness of the climb is clearly shown.
(Courtesy National Tramway Museum

Denby

Predecessors of the tramways described in this book were the early plateways built in the canal age. The Little Eaton Gangway, engineered by Benjamin Outram to the 3ft. 6in. gauge linked Denby Colliery to the Derby Canal. It opened in May 1795 and closed in July 1908.

Derby

The former county town of Derbyshire lying at the crossing of the Manchester - London and Birmingham-Leeds roads was a natural magnet for the early railways and became the hub of the Midland Railway. The Company built its locomotive works here and other industries were attracted, Rolls-Royce being the best known.

The Derby Tramways Co.Ltd. opened horse tramways in 1880 and eventually worked 23 double-deck horse cars on 4 miles of 4ft. gauge route from the Market Place to the Midland Station and along the London, Osmaston, Normanton and Ashbourne roads. The Corporation took over in 1899 and proceeded to electrify and extend the system.

The extended London Road and Osmaston Road routes were the first to be opened, on 27 July 1904, and others followed in 1905, 1907 and 1908 to give a total of eight routes. These followed all the generally wide main roads for up to two miles except those to the north. There was also a connecting service from the Midland Station to the Cavendish Hotel, crossing the London and Osmaston roads, before continuing via Normanton Road to the Market Place. The fleet eventually grew to 78 four-wheel cars of which four were single-deck to pass under a low bridge in Friargate. The trams were replaced during 1932-34 by trolleybuses and the last tram ran into Osmaston Road depot on 2 July 1934.

The Derby Tramways Company had a fleet of 23 double-deck horse tramcars. One is seen here serving the Ashbourne Road route. *(Courtesy of National Tramway Museum*

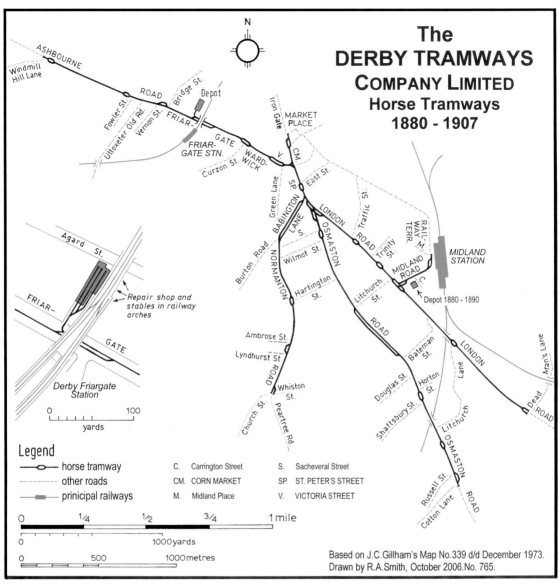

The DERBY TRAMWAYS
COMPANY LIMITED
Horse Tramways
1880 - 1907

Repair shop and stables in railway arches

Derby Friargate Station

0 ___ 100
yards

Legend

—○— horse tramway	C. Carrington Street	S. Sacheveral Street
------ other roads	CM. CORN MARKET	SP. ST. PETER'S STREET
▬▬ prinicipal railways	M. Midland Place	V. VICTORIA STREET

0   ¼   ½   ¾   1 mile

0   1000 yards

0   500   1000 metres

Based on J.C.Gillham's Map No.339 d/d December 1973.
Drawn by R.A.Smith, October 2006.No. 765.

The Brush Company supplied 25 open-top cars for the opening of the electric system in 1904. No 1 is seen at the Burton Road terminus.

(Commercial card courtesy National Tramway Museum

Telegraph poles and wires were a feature of most main roads out of the cities when electric tramways were built. Bracket arms were a feature of the Kedleston Road.   (W.W.Winter Commercial card courtesy National Tramway Museum

In the 1900's there was little traffic to disturb the pedestrians strolling along the London Road, which featured centre poles for the overhead wiring.   (Commercial card, courtesy National Tramway Museum

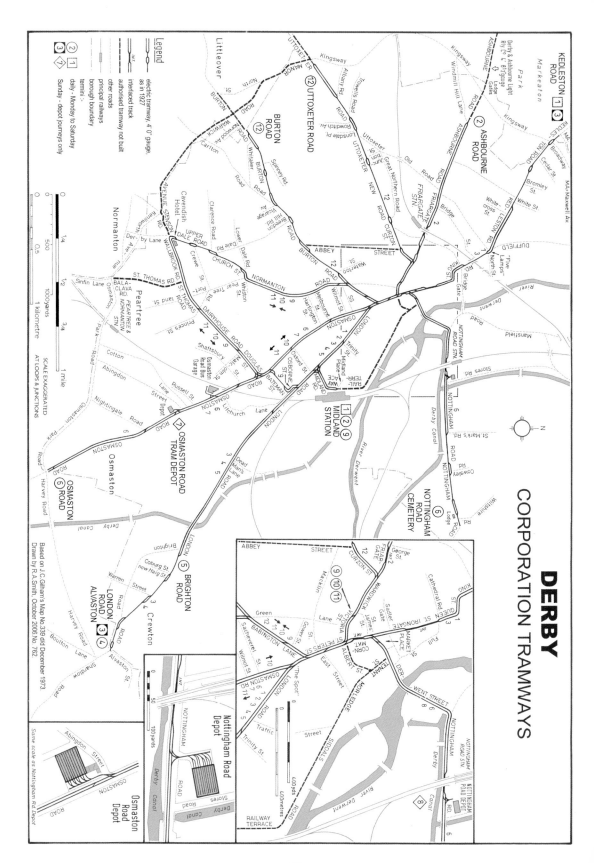

DERBY
CORPORATION TRAMWAYS

The majority of Derby tramcars were of the balcony type. No. 53 is seen among the trees on service 9 to Pear Tree. *(Courtesy National Tramway Museum*

The enclosed double deck tramcar came to Derby in 1925. The through service to Nottingham Road was discontinued on 14 November 1930 and service 6 then terminated at the Market Place where No 76 is waiting to depart for Osmaston Road, No. 66 is on Sunday service 3 to Kedleston Road. *(S.L.Smith, courtesy National Tramway Museum*

Ashbourne

A glance at the railway map will show that the town of Ashbourne, a centre for Dovedale, although only 13 miles north-west of Derby, was only accessible by rail via Burton-upon-Trent and Uttoxeter, a distance of 33 miles. It therefore attracted Crompton & Co.Ltd.,the famous Chelmsford electrical engineers, to seek powers for an electric tramway along the main road between the two towns. Although the gauge in the 1897 application was four feet, the Derby & Ashbourne Light Railway Company was authorised in 1901 to build 14 miles of 4ft.8$\frac{1}{2}$ in. line with presumably dual gauge within the city. None of this was ever built despite an announcement in 1908 that it was now "under construction". Maybe the promoters were put off by the lack of traffic potential: Ashbourne has a population of 5,500, an undulating road with a summit of 592 feet (180 meters) near Ashbourne and few settlements of any size between the termini.

Burton-upon-Trent

Eleven miles from Derby Midland station we reach Burton-upon-Trent famous for brewing based on local barley and pure water. As a result the town had a dense network of railways serving the breweries and there were no fewer than eight level crossings involving the electric tramways.

The electric tramway system was opened by the Corporation on 3 August 1903. There were over 6 miles of 3ft.6in.gauge. tracks, mostly single-line and loops, and services ran from Station Street north to Horninglow, south to Branston Road and over the Trent Bridge to Stapenhill and Winshill. They were operated by a fleet of 24 four-wheel cars, 14 open-top, ten with balcony covers, all built by Brush. The trams were closed down between 1927 and 1929, the last car running on 31 December.1929.

New Trent Bridge, Burton-on-Trent.

The bridge was widened in 1925, double-track replaced the single-line and loop and span wires the bracket arm poles. By this time six cars had received top covers and four new cars purchased. (*A.H. Taylor commercial card, courtesy National Tramway Museum*

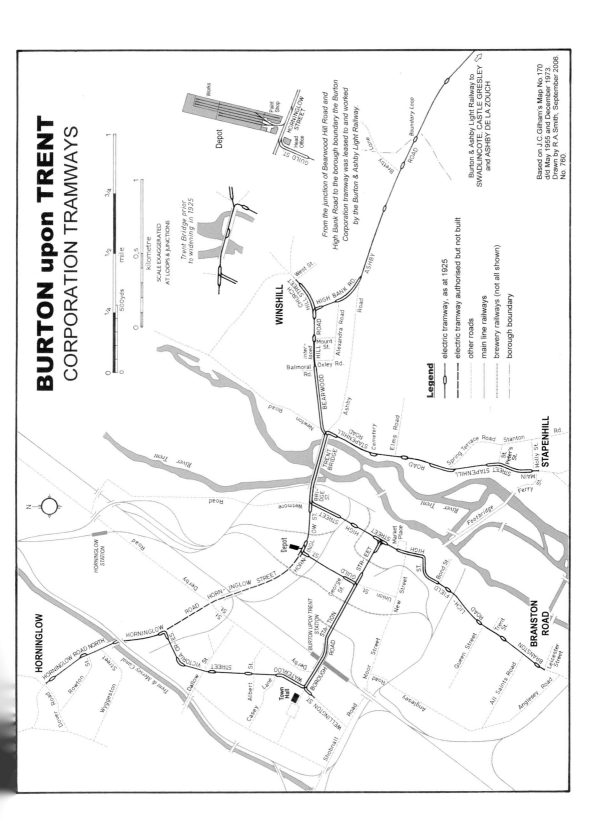

BURTON upon TRENT
CORPORATION TRAMWAYS

Depot

Works

Paint Shop

HORNINGLOW STREET

Head Office

GUILD ST

500yds

1/4 1/2 3/4 1 mile

kilometre

0,5 1

SCALE EXAGGERATED
AT LOOPS & JUNCTIONS

Trent Bridge prior
to widening in 1925

From the junction of Bearwood Hill Road and
High Bank Road to the borough boundary the Burton
Corporation tramway was leased to and worked
by the Burton & Ashby Light Railway.

WINSHILL

West St.

CHURCH HILL STREET

HIGH BANK RD.

ASHBY

ROAD

Road

Alexandra Road

Mount St.

inter-laced

Oxley Rd.

Balmoral Rd.

BEARWOOD

Ashby

Road

Newton

Ashby

Cemetery

Elms Road

STAPENHILL ROAD

TRENT BRIDGE

Spring Terrace Road

Stanton

STAPENHILL

ROAD

STAPENHILL MAIN STREET

Holly St.

St. Peter's St.

Ferry

River Trent

Footbridge

Rd.

Wetmore

Road

River Trent

BRIDGE ST.

HIGH STREET

STREET

Market Place

HIGH ST.

Bond St.

HORNINGLOW STATION

Road

Derby Road

HORN-INGLOW STREET

Depot

HORNINGLOW ST.

GUILD STREET

George St.

Union St.

New Street

Street

FIELD ST.

LICHFIELD ROAD

BRANSTON ROAD

HORNINGLOW

HORNINGLOW ROAD NORTH

St.

Rowton St.

VICTORIA CRES.

STREET

Dallow St.

Albert St.

Lane

WATERLOO

Derby St.

BURTON UPON TRENT STATION

STATION ROAD

BOROUGH

Town Hall

WELLINGTON ST.

Road

Shobnall Road

Moor Street

Road

Anglesey Road

Queen Street

All Saints Road

Trent St.

BRANSTON ROAD

Leicester Street

Anglesey Road

Wyggeston Street

Casey

Dover Road

Trent & Mersey Canal

HORNINGLOW

N

River Trent

Road

GUILD ST

Bretby Lane

ROAD

Boundary Loop

Burton & Ashby Light Railway to
SWADLINCOTE, CASTLE GRESLEY
and ASHBY DE LA ZOUCH

Based on J.C. Gilham's Map No.170
d/d May 1965 and December 1973.
Drawn by R.A. Smith, September 2006.
No. 760.

The Burton tram drivers had to negotiate at least two of the eight crossings on a journey to any terminus. No 2 is en route to Horninglow.   (Courtesy National Tramway Museum

Seen from the bridge over the Midland Railway No. 7 is proceeding up Borough Road with the Town Hall in the distance. The Station Hotel has since been renovated and converted to flats.   (John Mackie commercial card, courtesy National Tramway Museum

In addition to the Burton and Ashby service two Corporation services crossed the Trent Bridge to Stapenhill and Winshill respectively. Two open top cars are seen at the eastern end of the bridge circa 1908. *(Wrench series, courtesy National Tramway Museum*

Burton-on-Trent Corporation tramcar No.11 bound for Horninglow in High Street. In the left background another tram is turning into Station Street. *(National Tramway Museum*

There were lengths of single line on all the Burton routes. No 1 is on Bearwood Hill Road bound for Winshill. These tracks were also used by Burton and Ashby cars on their journey to the Burton terminus in Wellington Street. *(Commercial card, courtesy National Tramway Museum*

Burton and Ashby Light Railway

To the south of Burton and the Trent valley was undulating countryside overlying coal measures and fireclay, giving rise to numerous colliery villages and tile and pottery works in the Swadlincote area. This was served by a loop line off the rather indirect Burton - Ashby-de-la-Zouch line of the Midland Railway.

Agitation for a tramway to serve the area developed in the 1890's and eventually the Midland Railway obtained a Light Railway Order granted in 1902 for an electric tramway from the Burton boundary to Ashby via Newhall, Swadlincote and Woodville with a branch to Castle Gresley. The line was duly opened to Swadlincote on 13 June 1906 and to Ashby on 2 July.

The twenty open-top tramcars by Brush provided a forty minute service between the two towns with a connecting service to Castle Gresley. The trams ran over Burton Corporation tracks from Wellington Street past the Midland Station, over Trent Bridge and up the hill to the Borough boundary at Bretby Lane. Apart from 'the switchback' over the fields to Newhall the light railway, employing single track with loops controlled by lights, followed the local winding country roads through to Ashby. The link from Woodville to Church Gresley, was not remunerative and was withdrawn in 1912.

The ten-mile line, abandoned on 19 February 1927, provides the best example of a tramway owned by a main line railway company and the only example of railway-owned tramcars running on municipal tracks. The terminus tracks at Ashby Station are still in situ and tramcar No.14 was restored and operated in Detroit.

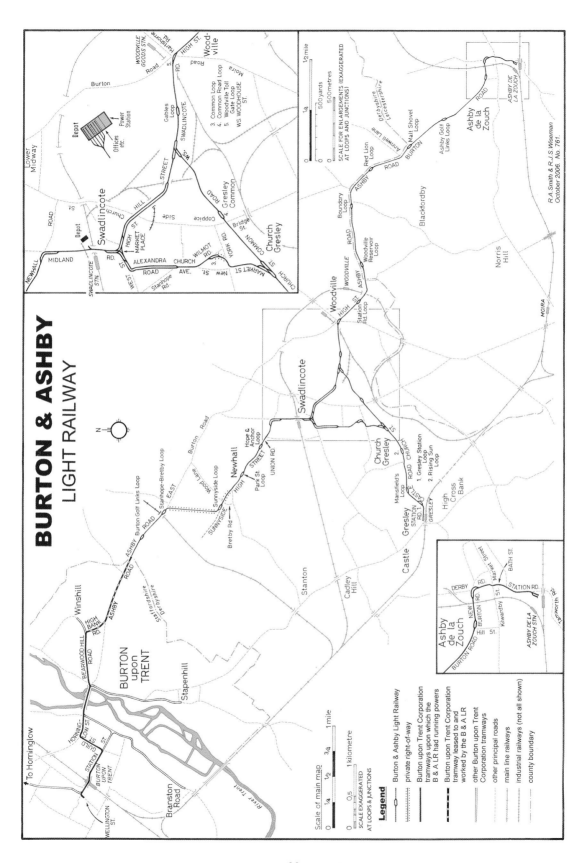

BURTON & ASHBY
LIGHT RAILWAY

R.A.Smith & R.J.S Wiseman
October 2006. No. 761.

Legend

Burton & Ashby Light Railway	
private right-of-way	
Burton upon Trent Corporation tramways upon which the B & A LR had running powers	
Burton upon Trent Corporation tramway leased to and worked by the B & A LR	
other Burton upon Trent Corporation tramways	
other principal roads	
main line railways	
industrial railways (not all shown)	
county boundary	

Scale of main map

0 ¼ ½ ¾ 1 mile

0 0.5 1 kilometre

SCALE EXAGGERATED AT LOOPS & JUNCTIONS

SCALE FOR ENLARGEMENTS (EXAGGERATED AT LOOPS AND JUNCTIONS)

½ mile ¼

500 yards

500metres

3. Common Loop
4. Common Road Loop
5. Woodville Toll Gate Loop
WS. WOODHOUSE ST.

The Burton and Ashby tramcars continued from Winshall junction on Corporation tracks in Ashby Road to the county boundary. A half mile further on the tracks went right on to a private track where we see No 5 heading for Newall and Swadlincote.   (Courtesy National Tramway Museum

No 20 also bound for Swadlincote has probably come from Castle Gresley and is seen at the York Road crossing with the Common loop round the corner to the left.   (R.B.Parr collection

The rural nature of the line is emphasised in this view of No 12 at Woodville. The locals seem more interested in the photographer rather than the tram.
(C. Lane, courtesy National Tramway Museum

Burton Road, Ashby-de-la-Zouch, a typical scene on the lengthy Burton and Ashby Tramway which was single track with passing loops except in the Swadlincote area. *(Valentine series Commercial card*

No 9 is about to negotiate the first loop after leaving Ashby Station at the corner of Derby Road and New Burton Road on its journey to Burton-on-Trent. The interested onlookers would appear to indicate this was probably opening day, 13 June 1905.   *(C. Lane, courtesy National Tramway Museum*

In the early years tramcar drivers had to contend with wandering pedestrians, cyclists and horse drawn vehicles. The driver of No.8 is making his way cautiously down Leeming Street towards the Market Place, Mansfield.   *(Jackson & Son, commercial card*

Mansfield

Returning north to Chesterfield we can follow the Great Central Railway south towards Nottingham, and by a change at Kirkby-in-Ashfield reach Mansfield. The town was an old market town and noted for its local stone quarries It developed rapidly as the local coalfield was exploited during the nineteenth century.and the Mansfield and Pinxton Tramway, built by Outram, was opened on 13 April 1819 to convey coal to the Cromford Canal. A horse tram operated on market days from 1832. The tramway was purchased by the Midland Railway and rebuilt for locomotive haulage.

Electric tramways were first proposed by local business men in November 1898 and a Light Railway Order for 5 miles of 3ft.8in.gauge electric tramways was obtained the following year. Extensions to Hucknall-under-Huthwaite and Pleasley, and a change of gauge to 4ft.8$\frac{1}{2}$ in., was obtained in February 1901.

The system was very extensive in proportion to the size of the town, with 12 route miles, and was opened in stages from 11 July 1905, concluding with that to Mansfield Woodhouse on 26 November 1907. Further extensions, including Crown Farm and Skegby were authorised in 1907, but only that to Crown Farm, serving Mansfield colliery, opened in 1905, was built and opened in April 1911. Further extensions to serve new colliery villages in Rainworth, Blidworth and Clipstone were authorised in 1920, but not one of these was built. The system was operated by the Mansfield and District Light Railway Company. The entire share capital was owned by the Mansfield and District Tramways Ltd, itself a subsidiary of the Midland Counties Electric Supply Company Ltd., owned by Balfour Beatty & Co.Ltd.

There were five routes, worked by 28 double-deck, four- wheel tramcars, radiating from the Market Place. The longest extending for over five miles, through Sutton-in-Ashfield to Huthwaite. The whole system was single-line and loops,except for a section of double, roadside reserved track, on Sutton Road built circa 1921. The Company changed its name to Mansfield District Traction Company and obtained an Act in 1929 to replace the trams with trolleybuses, but they gave way to motorbuses in the autumn of 1932.

The Market Place was the hub of the Mansfield system with services locally to Berry Hill, Crown farm, Mansfield Woodhouse and Pleasley and beyond Sutton-in Ashfield to Huthwaite. No 5, rebuilt in 1929 awaits departure to Berry Hill.
(Dr J. Nicol, courtesy National Tramway Museum

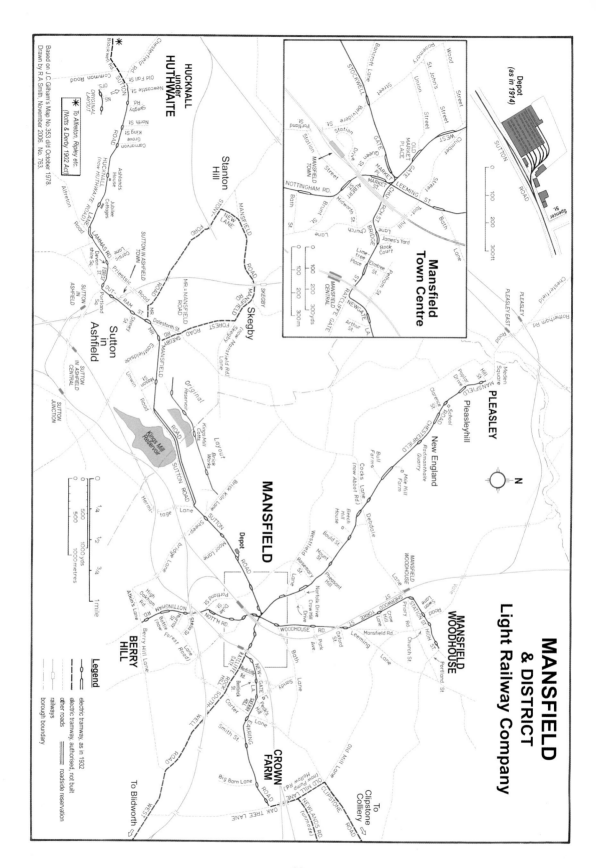

MANSFIELD & DISTRICT Light Railway Company

Mansfield Town Centre

Depot (as in 1914)

The service to Sutton-in-Ashfield was opened on 18 December 1906. No 17 was delivered from Brush the following year and is seen in Outram Street with cyclists and pedestrians predominating.
(Commercial card, courtesy National Tramway Museum

No 4 was fitted with a balcony top-covers c 1925. It is seen in High Street, Mansfield Woodhouse.
(Rex commercial card, courtesy National Tramway Museum

Mansfield Market Place was the hub of the system. In this view the Bentinck Memorial stands out above the market stalls. No 24 awaits departure with the Town Hall in the background.
(Rex series, courtesy National Tramway Museum

Looking in the opposite direction towards Leeming Street we see No 24 again many years later with the lower saloon showing signs of many years use.   (National Tramway Museum M.J.O'Connor

To the north-west the tram service extended almost three miles to Pleasley on the Derbyshire border and only nine miles from Chesterfield,. Except for the cyclist No 10 has a clear run on Chesterfield Road.
(Kingsway commercial card, courtesy National Tramway Museum

To the south the tramlines only extend a mile or so along the Nottingham Road to Berry Hill Lane where No 11 is waiting to return to town. *(Rex series courtesy National Tramway Museum*

Nottingham

The City of Nottingham has a history going back to Saxon times when a settlement developed close by a ford across the River Trent. The city gained a reputation for lace and hosiery during the eighteenth century and with the coming of canals and railways the city developed other industries and expanded northwards, expansion to the south being restricted by the River Trent.

The Nottingham and District Tramways Co.Ltd.introduced horse trams on 17 September 1878 and by the end of 1881 worked 7 miles of standard gauge route, including Carrington, Basford and Trent Bridge, with a mixture of double-deck and single-deck tramcars. On 16 October 1897 the Corporation purchased the Company tramways and continued to work them pending electrification. The first electric line, to Sherwood, opening on New Year's Day 1901. The spacious Market Place became the centre of the system, and although certain services started from Trent Bridge, lengthy routes extended out to Bulwell, Mapperley, Arnold and Carlton, the outer sections of the latter two were outside the city boundary and originally granted to the Notts & Derbys Company.

In 1920 the City planned many extensions including Beeston, Hucknall, and to the developing suburbs to the west of the city, but only short extensions to the Derby Road and Mapperley routes resulted. Similarly a new depot was built at Carter Gate and a new tracks laid in the Market Place in 1927, but the scheme was not completed.

The system was worked by a fleet of 200 double-deck cars, the majority single-truck; the last twenty purchased in 1926-27, eighteen of which ended their days in Aberdeen. The first trolleybuses were introduced in 1927 and replaced many of the routes, but the last two, Mapperley and Arnold were replaced by motorbuses.

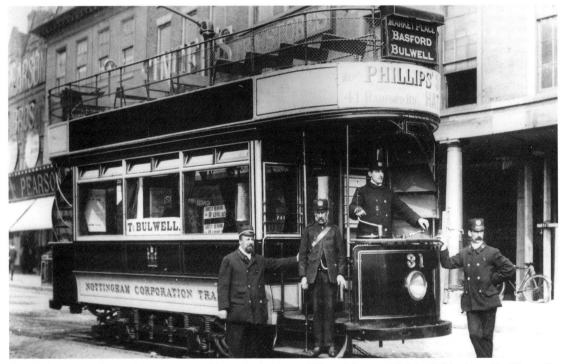

The Bulwell electric service was opened from the bottom of Chapel Bar on 23 July 1901 where No 31 awaits departure.   *(Courtesy National Tramway Museum*

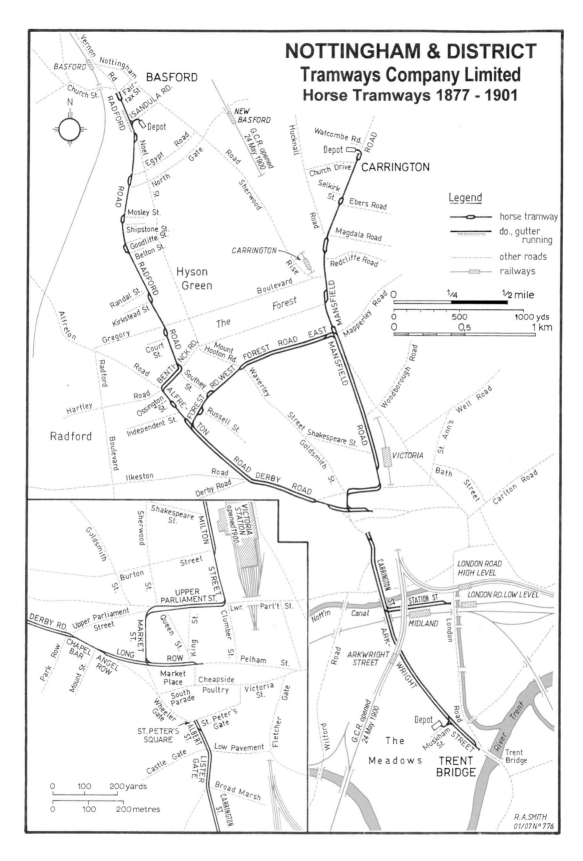

NOTTINGHAM & DISTRICT
Tramways Company Limited
Horse Tramways 1877 - 1901

Legend

- ○─○ horse tramway
- ─▨─ do., gutter running
- ----- other roads
- ─▨─ railways

R. A. SMITH
01/07 N° 776

Milnes horse Tram No. 37 on the Mansfield Road near Hucknall Road Junction. (National Tramway Museum

Nottingham Market Place viewed looking east towards the Council House. Three trams are in view on Long Row.   (Commercial card, courtesy National Tramway Museum

Basford Crossing, Nottingham

The Bulwell route passed through Basford and alongside the Midland Railway line to Mansfield. Nottingham Express Transit now shares the line as far as Hucknall. (*Commercial card courtesy National Tramway Museum*

The Market Place was renovated and the tram tracks relocated in 1929. The tram is on service 6 to Lenton. (*National Tramway Museum*

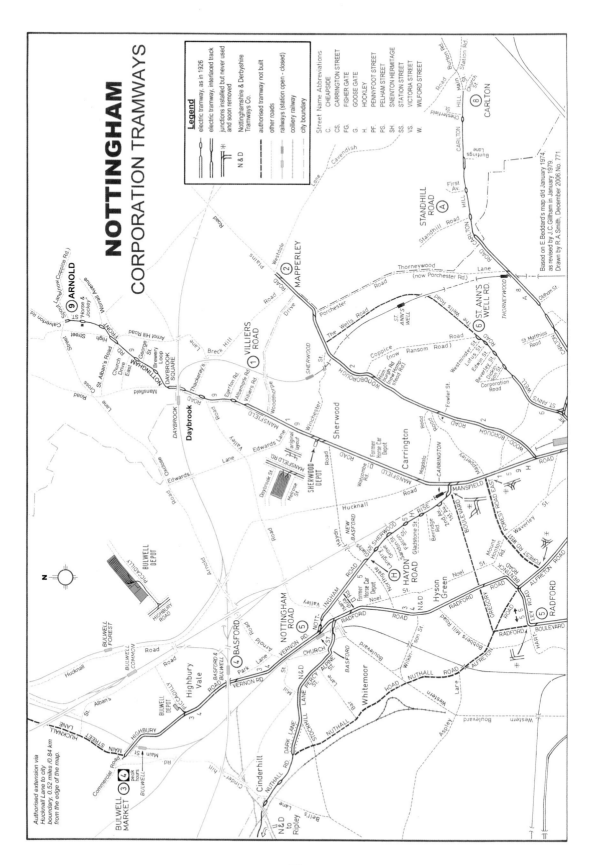

NOTTINGHAM
CORPORATION TRAMWAYS

Legend

	electric tramway, as in 1926
	electric tramway, interlaced track
	junctions installed but never used and soon removed
N & D	Nottinghamshire & Derbyshire Tramways Co.
	authorised tramway not built
	other roads
	railways (station open - closed)
	colliery railway
	city boundary

Street Name Abbreviations

C.	CHEAPSIDE
CS.	CARRINGTON STREET
FG.	FISHER GATE
GG.	GOOSE GATE
H.	HOCKLEY
PF.	PENNYFOOT STREET
PS.	PELHAM STREET
SH	SNEINTON HERMITAGE
SS.	STATION STREET
VS.	VICTORIA STREET
W.	WILFORD STREET

Based on E.Beddard's map d/d January 1974,
as revised by J.C.Gillham in January 1979.
Drawn by R.A.Smith, December 2006. No.771.

Authorised extension via
Hucknall Lane to city
boundary. 0.52 miles /0.84 km
from the edge of the map.

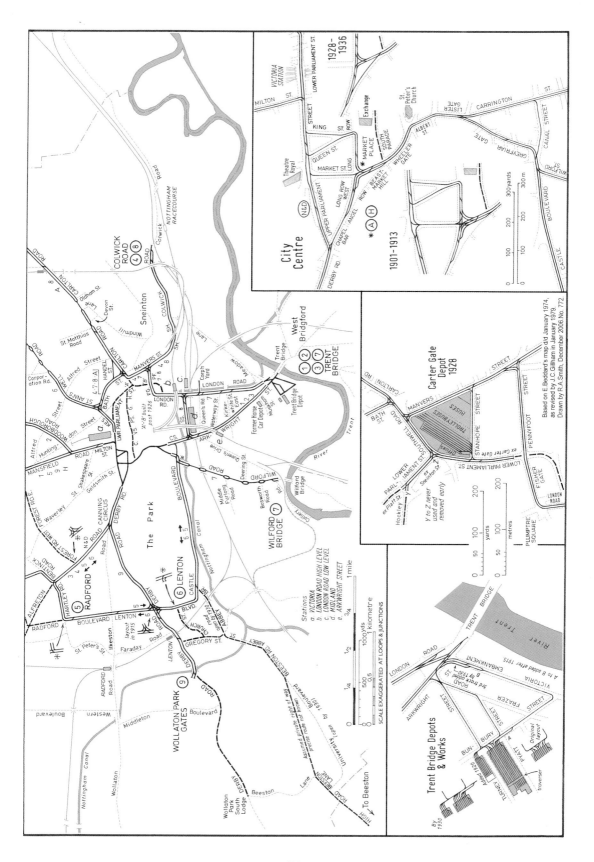

City Centre

1928 – 1936

VICTORIA STATION

MILTON ST.

LOWER PARLIAMENT ST

KING ST.

Exchange

St. Peter's Church

LISTER GATE

CARRINGTON ST.

CANAL STREET

Theatre Royal

QUEEN ST.

MARKET ST. LONG

MARKET PLACE

SOUTH PARADE

ALBERT ST.

WHEELER GATE

GREYFRIAR GATE

UPPER PARLIAMENT

LONG ROW WEST

LONG ROW

ANGEL ROW

BEAST-MARKET HILL

WILFORD ST.

BOULEVARD

CASTLE

DERBY RD.

CHAPEL BAR

(N&D)

1901–1913

(A) (H)

300 yards

300 m

200

200

100

100

0

0

Based on E Beddard's map d/d January 1974, as revised by J.C. Gillham in January 1979.
Drawn by R.A. Smith, December 2006. No. 772.

Carter Gate Depot 1928

CARLTON RD

STANHOPE STREET

MANVERS STREET

BATH ST.

SOUTHWELL ROAD

TROLLEYBUSES

BUSES

Offices

PENNYFOOT ST.

LOWER PARL-IAMENT ST.

ex Sneinton St

LOWER PARLIAMENT ST.

ex Carter Gate

FISHER GATE

LONDON ROAD

ex Platt St

Hockley

Y to Z never used and removed early

PLUMPTRE SQUARE

200

200

yards

metres

100

100

50

50

0

0

COLWICK ROAD (4)(8)

CARLTON ROAD A (8)

Oldham St.

Devon St.

St. Matthias Road

Windmill Lane

Sneinton

SH COLWICK

COLWICK ROAD

NOTTINGHAM RACECOURSE

West Bridgford

Trent Bridge

(1)(2)
(3)(7)

TRENT BRIDGE

Alfred Street

Corporation Rd.

HANDEL ST.

MANVERS ST.

4:7:8 A

St. ANN'S

WELLS ROAD

BATH STREET

4'8" built post 1926

LONDON RD.

Queen's Rd.

Waterway St.

Kirke-white St.

Mus. St.

LONDON ROAD

Former Horse Car Depot

Trent Bridge Depot

Trent

River

WOODBOROUGH ROAD

MANSFIELD ROAD

MILTON ST.

ROBIN HOOD ST.

Alfred Street

Hunting St.

LWR. PARLIAMENT

ARKWRIGHT ST.

Queens Drive

Deering St.

Middle Furlong Road

Bosworth Road

Wilford Bridge

WILFORD ROAD

Colliery

WILFORD BRIDGE (7)

Shakespeare St.

Goldsmith St.

FOREST RD.E.

FOREST RD WEST

N&D

CANNING CIRCUS

DERBY ROAD

The Park

Nottingham Canal

Stations
a. VICTORIA
b. LONDON ROAD HIGH LEVEL
c. LONDON ROAD LOW LEVEL
d. MIDLAND
e. ARKWRIGHT STREET

Waverley St.

RADFORD (5)

LENTON (6)

CASTLE BLVD.

ALFRETON ROAD

BENTINCK ROAD

HARTLEY ROAD

RADFORD ROAD

ABBEY ST.

DERBY ROAD

BOULEVARD LENTON

GREGORY ST.

St. Peter's St.

Faraday Road

Ilkeston Road

LENTON

ABBEY ST.

CHURCH ST.

BEESTON RD

road 1930 open by

layout in 1915

RADFORD (open by 1930)

Assumed private right of way (precise route not known)

University (open by 1930)

WOLLATON PARK GATES (9)

DERBY ROAD

Western Boulevard

Middleton Boulevard

Wollaton

Nottingham Canal

Wollaton Park South Lodge

BEESTON LANE

DERBY ROAD

Beeston

HIGH

To Beeston

1 mile

3/4

1/2

1/4

100 yds

500

1 kilometre

0.5

1/4

SCALE EXAGGERATED AT LOOPS & JUNCTIONS

Trent Bridge Depots & Works

TRENT BRIDGE

River Trent

LONDON ROAD

ARKWRIGHT STREET

FRAZER ST.

VICTORIA STREET

EMBANKMENT

3rd track added by 1930

BUN-BURY ST.

TURNEY ST.

A to B added after 1915

By 1930

Added 1920

A

PLATT

Original layout

Traverser

The Walter Fountain where the Trent Bridge route via Carrington Street and the Midland Station to the right diverged from the Wilford Bridge route via Greyfriars Gate to the left.
(J.W.Rudduck & Sons commercial card, courtesy National Tramway Museum

Passengers are boarding No.41 at the corner of the Old Market Square. It appears to be an extra working to Trent Bridge to serve a match. Note the number screen displays Football Ground.
(National Tramway Museum

The junction of Mansfield Road and Gregory Boulevard is where the Nottingham Road service diverged to the left. The Notts & Derbys trolleybuses were routed this way when the tram service was discontinued.   *(Clumber series, courtesy National Tramway Museum*

Balcony car No 138 at Mapperley terminus was twenty years old at the time of the photograph in June 1934. Route letters replaced route numbers on 5 March 1933. No 138 would be on service B to the Old Market Square, Service A to Trent Bridge having been abandoned on 12 May 1934.   *(M.J.O'Connor, National Tramway Museum*

The Library Loop, Arnold, where it all began. My grandmother's shop was on the left and my brother and I could watch the trams pass in the loop. In 1937 they were no longer and we asked why? No 97 is seen outside the shop where this card was discovered.

(Rex series, commercial card

Arnold terminus with Brush balcony car No 146 of 1914 shimmering in the sunshine.

(National Tramway Museum

In June 1935 No 195 was photographed at Worral Avenue loop, Arnold.

(R.B.Parr, National Tramway Museum

Ilkeston Corporation 5 and 6 at the last loop before Hallam Fields terminus, 16 May 1903, the opening day. Did they celebrate to the same extent on the last day?

(National Tramway Museum

Ilkeston

The small manufacturing town of Ilkeston, population 32,000, on the Derbyshire side of the River Erewash and seven miles from Nottingham opened a small 3 mile 3ft. 6in. gauge corporation tramway system on 16 May 1903, from Cotmanhay through the centre of the town to Hallam Fields close by the Stanton Ironworks. There was also a short branch to Ilkeston Junction Station on the Midland Main Line. Thirteen four-wheel open-top trams were needed, and operation was taken over by the Notts & Derby Company in 1916.

In 1922 the Notts & Derby Company purchased the Ilkeston system and obtained powers to build a tramway link from Ilkeston to their line at Heanor and also to change the gauge to standard, but these powers were never exercised. Instead the Company replaced the trams by motor buses early in 1931 and trolleybuses a year later which ran through to Heanor by the direct route.

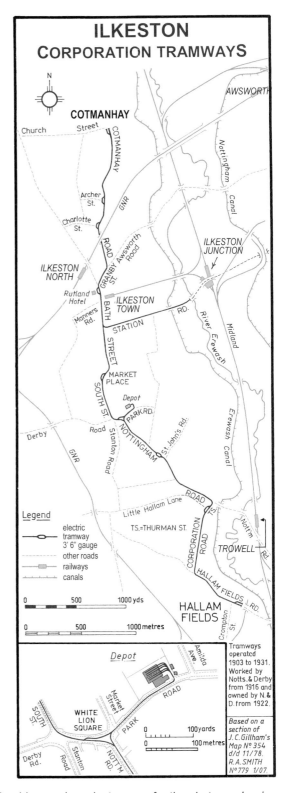

The driver and conductor pose for the photographer in Ilkeston No. 4.   *(National Tramway Museum*

Preston built No. 6 with an early type of lifeguard stands majestically at the Hallam Fields Terminus. *(National Tramway Museum*

A lonely tram makes its way down the single-track between the shops of Bath Street Ilkeston. *(Commercial card, courtesy National Tramway Museum*

Nottinghamshire & Derbyshire Coalfield

This extensive coalfield initially developed along the Erewash Valley and over the years extended eastwards to the north of Nottingham giving rise to a network of mining settlements intermixed with the older villages. Although the area was well served by a network of railways developed by the Midland, Great Northern and Great Central Companies. A number of tramway promoters were attracted and the following Light Railway schemes were applied for in November 1901.

Erewash Valley **Light Railway**	18 miles, standard gauge. Alfreton, Ripley, Heanor, Cinderhill with a branch from Heanor through Ilkeston to Trowell with mixed gauge in Ilkeston.
Derby and Nottingham **Light Railways**.	14 miles, standard; 5 miles 3ft.6in. gauge. Long Eaton, Sandiacre, Trowell Ilkeston. Long Eaton, Borrowash, Chaddesden to the Derby system. Long Eaton, Chilwell, Beeston, Lenton, to the Nottingham system
Mansfield and District **Light Railway Company**	21$\frac{1}{4}$ miles, 3ft.6in.gauge. Extensions to Huthwaite, Alfreton, Ripley, Belper, Duffield, also Ripley, Heanor, Ilkeston.
Derby, Nottingham and **District Light Rail Company**	24$\frac{3}{4}$ miles, standard gauge. Alfreton and Swanwick to Pye Bridge. Belper, to Duffield to join the Derby system. Also Trowell to Nottingham; and Sandiacre to Beeston.
Nottingham Suburban	11 Miles, Standard gauge. Extensions of Corporation system, Arnold, Carlton and Hucknall Torkhard.

These schemes totalled 94 miles of track and the proposed tramways would have linked Derby with Nottingham and Alfreton, and also with with the Mansfield lines. These four schemes were superseded and completely overshadowed by the 1902 Bill of the Nottinghamshire and Derbyshire Tramways Company, owned by the Midland Counties Electric Supply Co.Ltd. The Bill asked for 79 miles of standard gauge electric tramway, divided into 42 sections as shown on the accompanying map. It was a single track system with 316 passing loops totalling 13 miles.

Not surprisingly the Midland Railway Company objected to tramways linking Derby with Long Eaton and Nottingham and as a result these routes were deleted and only 39 miles were authorised in the 1903 Act. Of these eight miles were taken over by Nottingham Corporation in 1911, 19 miles abandoned and only 11 miles, Ripley to Cinderhill actually constructed.

The opening date is in some doubt, but is believed to have been Kimberley to Crosshills, near Codnor, on 29 July 1913, to Cinderhill 7 August and to Ripley on 15 August. The service ran through to Nottingham via Basford and not via Nuthall Road as originally proposed. There were 24 four-wheeled cars which ran through to Parliament Street, Nottingham; from Cinderhill over one mile leased from the Corporation and finally two miles, exercising running powers from Basford into the city centre. This was the longest privately run tram service in the country, although the Glasgow Corporation Service from Milngavie to Renfrew Ferry at 22 miles was longer. The Company promoted a Bill in 1922 to revive the two miles Heanor-Ilkeston direct

Sheffield 264 was a late arrival at Crich and is seen parked in the approaches to the depot.

(R.J.S.Wiseman

Sheffield 74 went to Gateshead in 1922 and its lower saloon came to Crich in Spring 1991. It had been fully restored by 1995 and is seen in the town with the Red Lion in the background.   (R.J.S.Wiseman

Edinburgh 35 was built in 1948 and is on loan from the city and was photographed on the depot fan on 5 August 2000. *(R.J.S.Wiseman*

The Glasgow Corporation tram was one of the finest double-deckers ever built. No 1282 is seen at Wakebridge with Southampton 45 and Metropolitan Feltham No 331 behind. *(R.J.S.Wiseman*

No. 106 a London County Council Class B tram dating from 1903 served as a snowbroom until 1952. It was restored by the LCC Tramways Trust and is seen at Crich on 17 May 2003.   (R.J.S.Wiseman

Newcastle Corporation No.102 dates from 1902 and seating 92 passengers was popular on race meetings days at Gosforth Park. It is about to return to the depot.   (R.J.S.Wiseman

Liverpool opened its Edge Lane Works in 1928 and built trams there until 1942. Bogie Streamliner No. 869 was built there in 1936 and after service in Glasgow now operates at Crich and is seen at Town End terminus on 3 June 1996. *(R.J.S.Wiseman*

Arriving at Town End are London Transport 1622 followed by Southampton 45 and Gateshead 5. 29 August 1998. *(R.J.S.Wiseman*

The new tramway enters the city via Market Street where No. 210 is seen on the opening day, 9 March 2004. The Theatre Royal is in the background. (R.J.S. Wiseman

The branch to Phoenix Park was laid on the track bed that served Cinderhill Colliery. No. 211 is at the terminus also on 9 March 2004. (R.J.S. Wiseman

The level crossing at David Lane on the NET system is unique because the light rail is protected by the traffic signals as part of the pre-existing road junction, while the parallel heavy rail Robin Hood line is protected by traditional railway flashing lights and barriers.
(S. Smiler

There is a three track layout at the Forest Park & Ride stop. This stop will be busiest during the Goose Fair held on the Forest each October. *(R.J.S. Wiseman*

No. 213 in bright blue advertising livery at the Hucknall terminus on 9 March 2004 the first day of public service. *(R.J.S. Wiseman*

No. 202 at the Old Market Square awaits departure for Station Street also on 9 March 2004.

(R.J.S. Wiseman

There are ten tramcars from outside the British Isles in the Crich collection. Prague 180, posed at Town End on 20 February 1996, was delivered to Crich in 1968. *(R.J.S. Wiseman*

There are seven Sheffield trams in the Crich collection The first to arrive and the inspiration for the Crich site was '1927 Standard' car No. 189 which arrived on 28 October 1960. It is seen in the depot alongside No. 330 which arrived some time later. *(R.J.S. Wiseman*

tramway, as noted above, but this was not built. The tramway continued operating its trams for a further twelve years and although efforts were made to attract passengers by painting some cars in a bright green livery and lowering fares closure was inevitable. The last car ran on 31 December 1932, although a morning and evening workman's service is said to have run between Heanor and Cinderhill until the through trolleybus service began on 6 October 1933.

The Nottingham terminus was in Upper Parliament Street where we find balcony car No 16 awaiting departure for Ripley almost 13 miles away. (National Tramway Museum

Beyond the city boundary the route was up and down the hills and this view of Hill Top, Eastwood is typical of the scenery. (Rex commercial card, courtesy National Tramway Museum

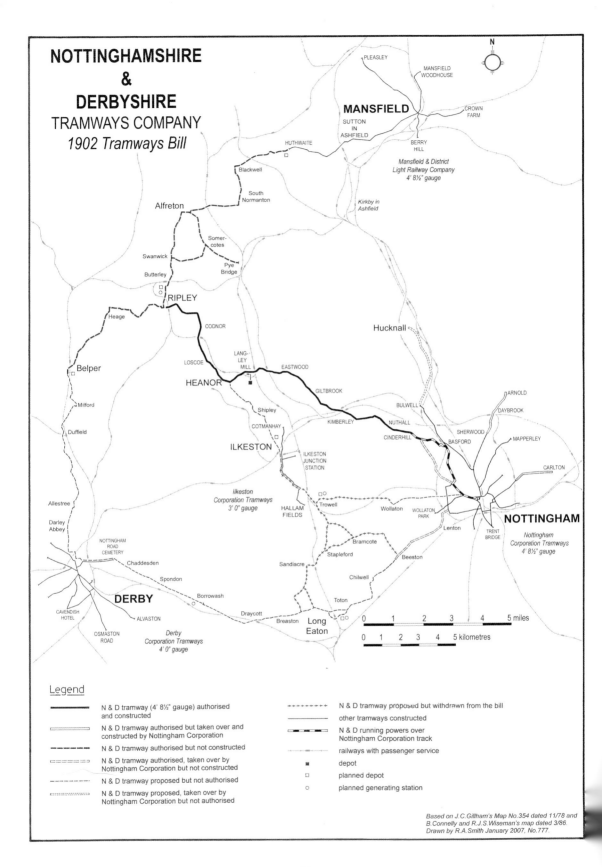

NOTTINGHAMSHIRE
&
DERBYSHIRE
TRAMWAYS COMPANY
1902 Tramways Bill

N

PLEASLEY

MANSFIELD
WOODHOUSE

MANSFIELD

CROWN
FARM

SUTTON
IN
ASHFIELD

HUTHWAITE

BERRY
HILL

Mansfield & District
Light Railway Company
4' 8½" gauge

Blackwell

South
Normanton

Kirkby in
Ashfield

Alfreton

Somer-
cotes

Swanwick

Pye
Bridge

Butterley

RIPLEY

Heage

CODNOR

Hucknall

Belper

LOSCOE

LANG-
LEY
MILL

EASTWOOD

ARNOLD

Milford

HEANOR

GILTBROOK

BULWELL

DAYBROOK

Duffield

Shipley

KIMBERLEY

NUTHALL

SHERWOOD

MAPPERLEY

COTMANHAY

CINDERHILL

BASFORD

ILKESTON

ILKESTON
JUNCTION
STATION

CARLTON

Allestree

Ilkeston
Corporation Tramways
3' 0" gauge

Trowell

HALLAM
FIELDS

Wollaton

WOLLATON
PARK

NOTTINGHAM

Darley
Abbey

NOTTINGHAM
ROAD
CEMETERY

Lenton

TRENT
BRIDGE

Nottingham
Corporation Tramways
4' 8½" gauge

Chaddesden

Bramcote

Spondon

Stapleford

Beeston

Sandiacre

Chilwell

DERBY

Borrowash

Toton

CAVENDISH
HOTEL

ALVASTON

Draycott

Breaston

Long
Eaton

OSMASTON
ROAD

Derby
Corporation Tramways
4' 0" gauge

| 0 | 1 | 2 | 3 | 4 | 5 miles |

| 0 | 1 | 2 | 3 | 4 | 5 kilometres |

Legend

■■■	N & D tramway (4' 8½" gauge) authorised and constructed	
▭▭▭	N & D tramway authorised but taken over and constructed by Nottingham Corporation	
▬ ▬ ▬	N & D tramway authorised but not constructed	
▭=▭=▭	N & D tramway authorised, taken over by Nottingham Corporation but not constructed	
─ ─ ─	N & D tramway proposed but not authorised	
▭▭▭▭	N & D tramway proposed, taken over by Nottingham Corporation but not authorised	

+++++++	N & D tramway proposed but withdrawn from the bill
────	other tramways constructed
▬█▬█▬	N & D running powers over Nottingham Corporation track
─··─	railways with passenger service
■	depot
▢	planned depot
○	planned generating station

Based on J.C.Gillham's Map No.354 dated 11/78 and
B.Connelly and R.J.S.Wiseman's map dated 3/86.
Drawn by R.A.Smith January 2007, No.777.

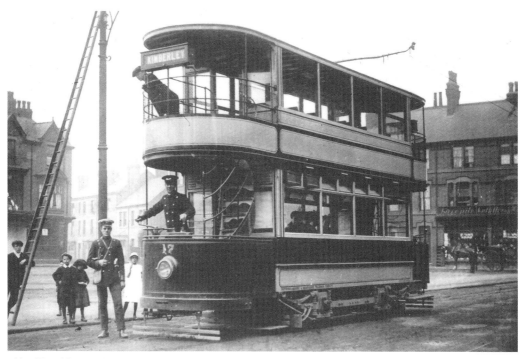

No 17 at Heanor Market Place shows Kimberley on the destination screen. This suggests that the service had not yet extended into Nottingham. (National Tramway Museum

A crowd surrounds No 14 at Loscoe loop prior to the opening of the service. (National Tramway Museum

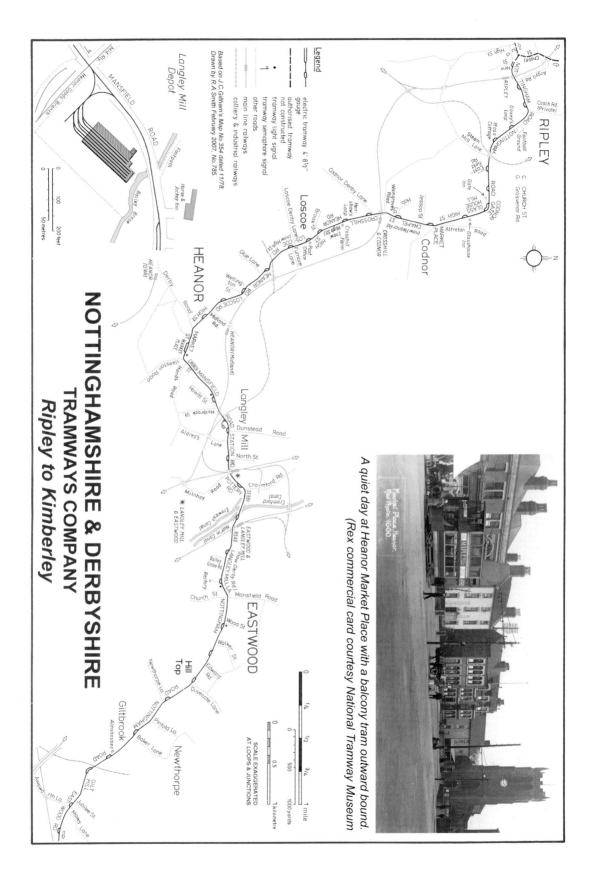

NOTTINGHAMSHIRE & DERBYSHIRE
TRAMWAYS COMPANY
Ripley to Kimberley

Legend

electric tramway 4' 8½" gauge
authorised tramway not constructed
tramway light section
tramway semaphore signal
other roads
main line railways
colliery & industrial railways

Based on J.C.Gillham's Map No.354 dated 11/78
Drawn by R.A.Smith February 2007, No.785

RIPLEY

C CHURCH ST.
G Grosvenor Rd.

Langley Mill Depot

Codnor

Loscoe

HEANOR

Langley Mill

EASTWOOD

Hill Top

Newthorpe

Giltbrook

A quiet day at Heanor Market Place with a balcony tram outward bound.
(Rex commercial card courtesy National Tramway Museum)

SCALE EXAGGERATED
AT LOOPS & JUNCTIONS

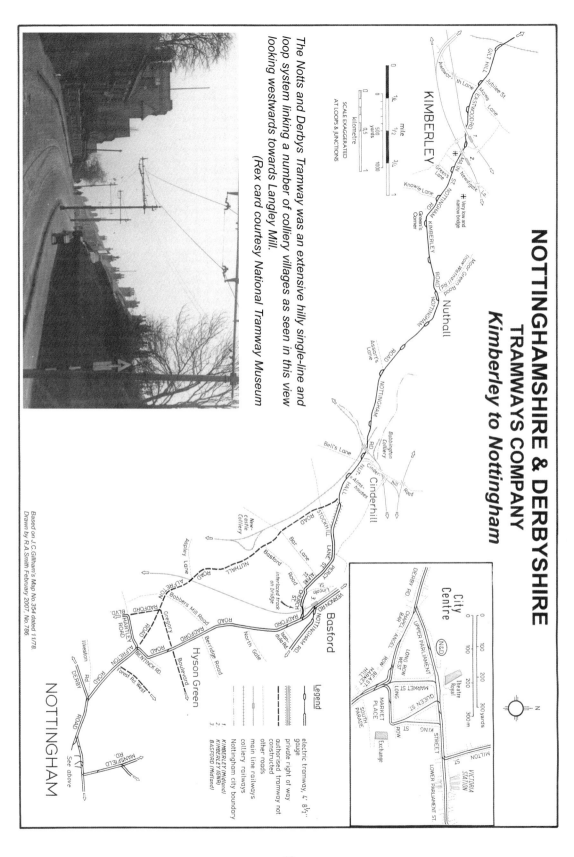

NOTTINGHAMSHIRE & DERBYSHIRE
TRAMWAYS COMPANY
Kimberley to Nottingham

The Notts and Derbys Tramway was an extensive hilly single-line and loop system linking a number of colliery villages as seen in this view looking westwards towards Langley Mill.

(Rex card courtesy National Tramway Museum)

KIMBERLEY

SCALE EXAGGERATED
AT LOOPS & JUNCTIONS

Nuttall

Cinderhill

Basford

Hyson Green

NOTTINGHAM

City Centre

Legend

electric tramway, 4' 8½" gauge
private right of way
authorised tramway not constructed
other roads
main line railways
Nottingham city boundary
colliery railways

1 KIMBERLEY (Midland)
2 KIMBERLEY (GNR)
3 BASFORD (Midland)

Based on J C Gillham's Map No.354 dated 11/78
Drawn by R.A.Smith February 2007, No.786

No 19 at Ripley terminus by the Ebenezer Chapel.
(M.J. O'Connor National Tramway Museum

Nottingham Express Transit

Moving forward a century we find that trams have returned to Nottingham, to a part of the system proposed in 1901. It is also to be hoped that trams will finally run to some of the other destinations proposed by the early promoters.

Proposals for the new tramway system first saw the light of day in 1989 and the Bill for the line from the Midland Station to Hucknall, with a branch to Phoenix Park received the Royal Assent in July 1994. The first street tracks were laid in Noel Street on 26 November 2001 passenger services opened on 9 March 2004.

The new line, nine miles, is worked by 15 Bombardier Incentro trams built at Derby and runs alongside the Robin Hood railway from Wilkinson Street to Hucknall; the branch to Phoenix Park is on the course of an old colliery line to Cinderhill. Future extensions are due to be constructed to Clifton and Chilwell via Beeston.

No 207 on trial at David's Lane 16 March 2003. *(R.J.S. Wiseman*

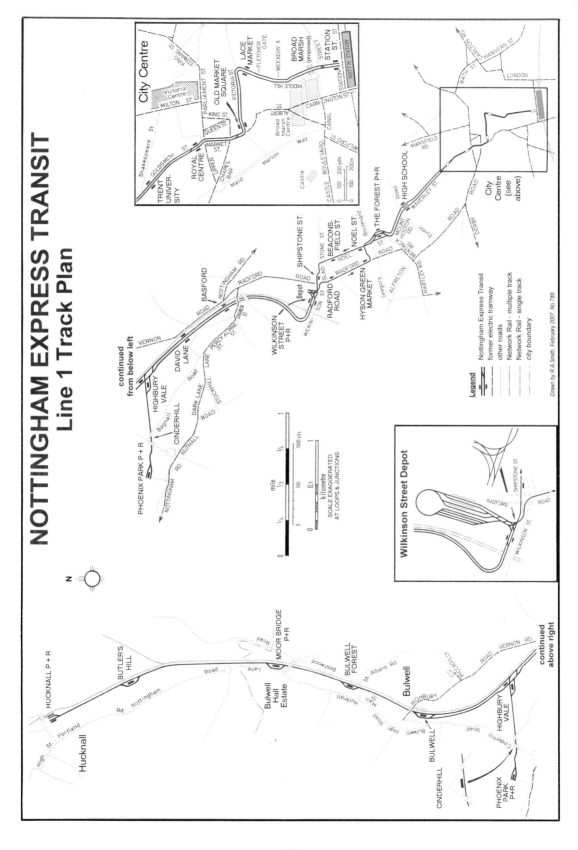

NOTTINGHAM EXPRESS TRANSIT
Line 1 Track Plan

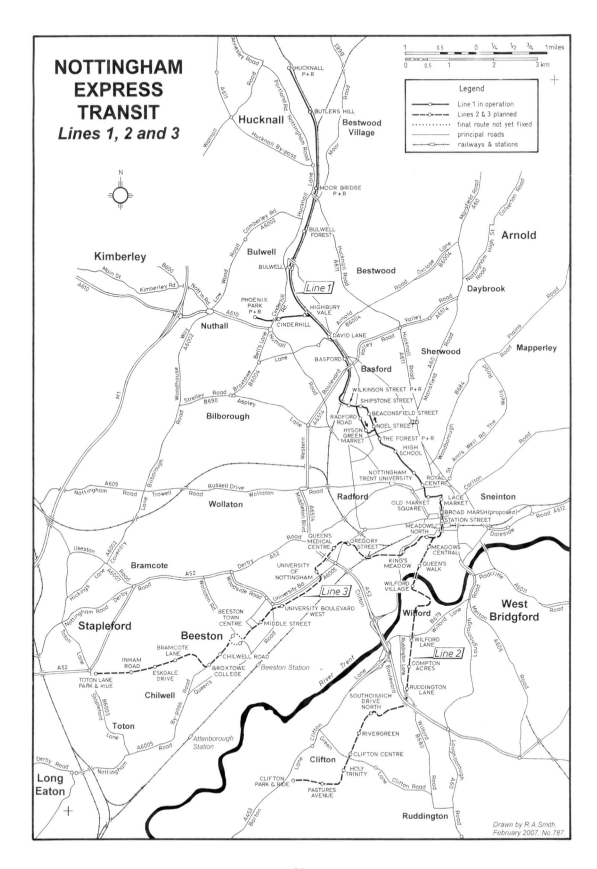

NOTTINGHAM EXPRESS TRANSIT
Lines 1, 2 and 3

Loughborough

Continuing south following the Midland Railway from Ilkeston or the Great Central from Nottingham we reach Loughborough. The town has engineering works, the best known being the Falcon Works established in 1865 by Henry Hughes to build steam tram engines. The Brush Electrical Engineering Co.Ltd. was established in 1889 and took over the Falcon works, which over the years produced around 8,000 tramcars ranging from the open top cars for Derby in 1904 to the excellent Middleton bogie cars for Leeds in 1935. The works had an extensive dual-gauge test track,in the form of a continuous loop including an artificial hill and a long branch constructed in 1901.

It is interesting to speculate that if the Loughborough system had been built would the Brush Company have tested its trams on the tracks that would have served the Brush works?

The Loughborough and District Electric Traction Co. Ltd., received powers in 1901 to build 6 miles of 3ft.6in. gauge tramway in the town. Unfortunately the main line from Hathern along the A6 road through the town to Mountsorrel, together with two short branches, were never built.

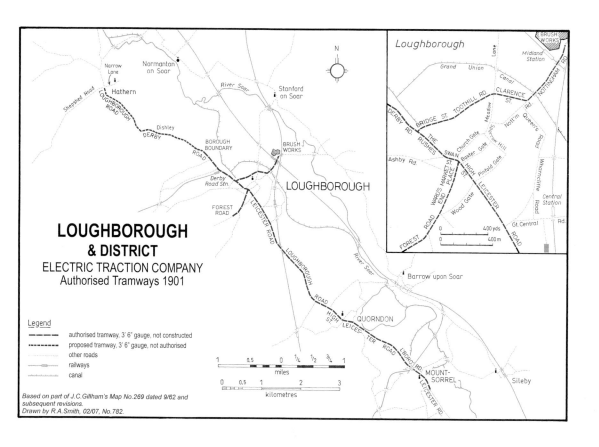

Leicester

The city of Leicester situated on the Fosse Way, has a history going back to before the Roman Era. Later it developed footwear and hosiery industries followed by engineering during the last century. The Leicester Tramways Company was formed in 1872, opened in 1875, and 46 horse trams were running over nine miles of standard gauge tracks, when taken over by the Corporation in June 1901.

The Corporation built up a compact traditional electric tramway system of eleven routes radiating from the complex junctions at the Clock Tower, the first being opened on 18 May 1904 between Stoneygate and Belgrave. Extensions were authorised but only the lines to Clarendon Park via Welford Road, Blackbird Road on reserved sleeper tracks and on Coleman Road branch, opened in 1927, were built. The city was served by a fleet of 178 double-deck four-wheel trams built between 1903 and 1920, all except for six were latterly top covered. Leicester had a highly developed fare and ticket system and at one time experimented with a penny flat fare.

The Melbourne Road service with its single track and loops, was abandoned in 1933, but all the trunk routes survived to the post war era and were abandoned in 1947-49, the last car, No.58 ran to Humberstone on 9 November 1949.

In 1904 6¼ miles of 4ft.8½ in. electric tramway was authorised to Colonel Crompton of Chelmsford as The Leicester, Anstey, Groby and Newton Linford Light Railway, a line initially sponsored In 1899 by Power & Traction Ltd. Although Crompton & Co.Ltd. formed a new subsidiary, The Railways and Tramways Corporation Ltd.to take over both this project and the Derby-Ashbourne line, neither were built.

The Leicester Tramways Company's fleet of horse trams was taken over by the Corporation in June 1901. The crew of No 9 and the horse appear to have been posed for the photograph.
(National Tramway Museum

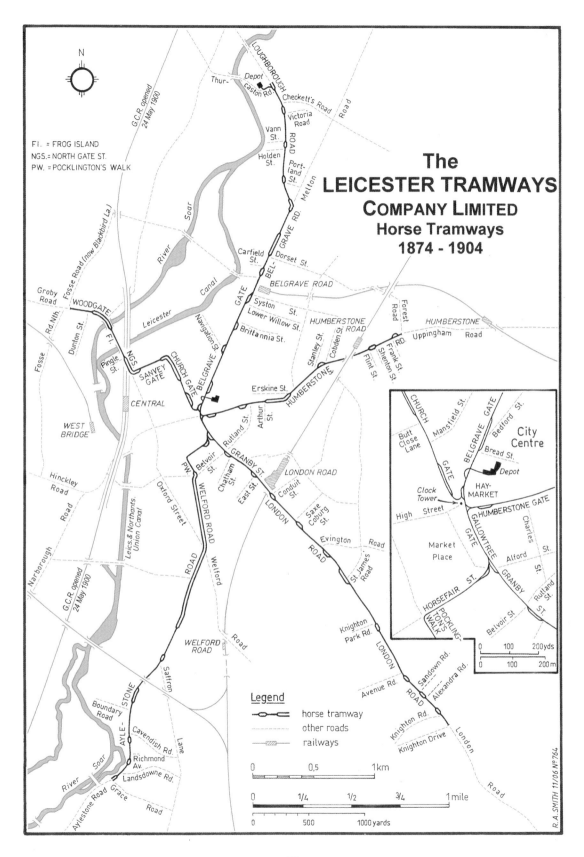

The LEICESTER TRAMWAYS COMPANY LIMITED
Horse Tramways
1874 - 1904

Fl. = FROG ISLAND
NGS.= NORTH GATE ST.
PW. = POCKLINGTON'S WALK

Legend

○—○	horse tramway
- - -	other roads
▨▨	railways

R.A. SMITH 11/06 Nº 764

All electric services except 5 Aylestone and 6 Clarendon Park passed by the Clock Tower. No 144 on service 3 from Fosse Road to Stoneygate is turning right from High Street into Gallowgate on 23 June 1937.
(National Tramway Museum, H.B. Priestley

Congestion in High Street Leicester with tram No 80 competing with a variety of vehicles, Interestingly the vehicle in the foreground was registered in Sheffield.
(Commercial card, courtesy National Tramway Museum

The Narborough Road diverged left from the Hinkley Road at Braunstone Gate. An open-top tram, possibly No 46 is heading towards the city. Note the ornate centre poles initially used to support the overhead. *(Commercial card, courtesy National Tramway Museum*

There was a siding in Humberstone Gate the terminus for services 7 and 8 to Humberstone and Coleman Road. Services 1 and 2 also passed this way on 23 June 1937. No 28 is for Western Park and No 132 is for East Park Road. *(H.B.Priestley, National Tramway Museum*

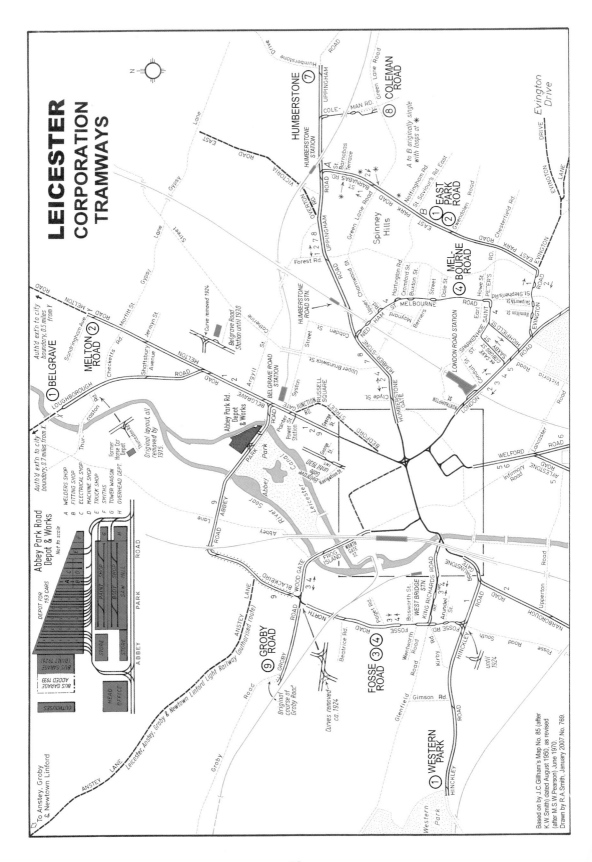

LEICESTER CORPORATION TRAMWAYS

Abbey Park Road Depot & Works
Not to scale

A WELDERS SHOP
B FITTING SHOP
C ELECTRICAL SHOP
D MACHINE SHOP
E TRUCK SHOP
F SMITHS
G TOWER WAGON
H OVERHEAD DEPT.

DEPOT FOR 153 CARS
BUS GARAGE (BUILT 1926)
BUS GARAGE ADDED 1933
OUTHOUSES

STORE
PAINT SHOP
BODY SHOP
SAW MILL
STORE
HEAD OFFICE

Based on by J.C. Gillham's Map No. 85 (after
K.W.Smith) dated August 1950, as revised
(after M.S.W.Pearson) June 1970.
Drawn by R.A.Smith, January 2007 No. 769.

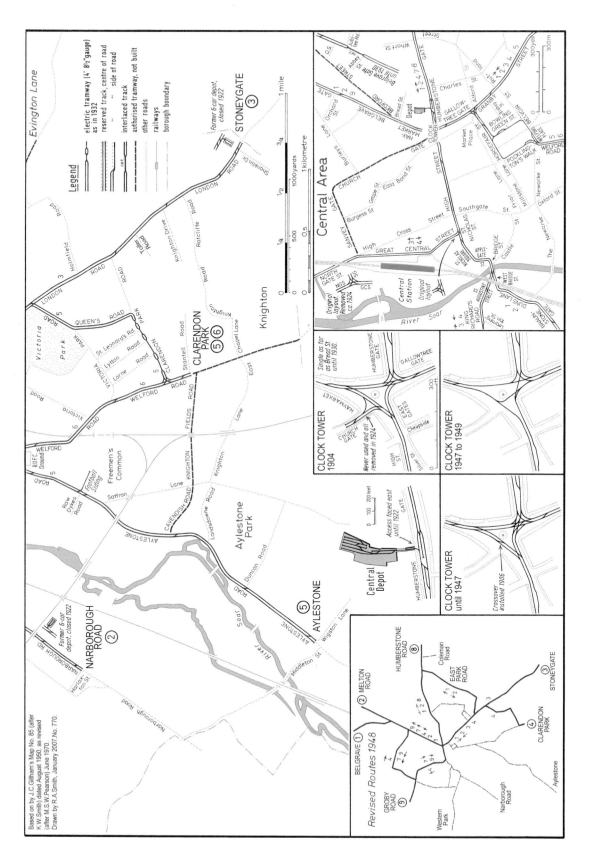

Legend

electric tramway (4′ 8½″gauge) as in 1932
reserved track, centre of road
         "   "   side of road
interlaced track
authorised tramway, not built
other roads
railways
borough boundary

Evington Lane

STONEYGATE ③
Former 6-car depot, closed 1922

London Road
Shanklin Dr.
Knighton Drive
Ratcliffe Road
Toller Road
Holmfield Road
London Road
Victoria Park Road
QUEEN'S ROAD
St. Leonard's Rd.
Lytton Road
Lorne Road
CLARENDON PARK ROAD
Stanfell Road
Chapel Lane
Knighton
CLARENDON PARK ⑤⑥
WELFORD ROAD
Knighton

Victoria Park

Victoria Road
Victoria Park Road

WELFORD ROAD
R.U.F.C. Ground
Football Siding
Freemen's Common
Saffron Lane
Landsdowne Road
CAVENDISH ROAD
KNIGHTON
Knighton Lane
FIELDS ROAD
East

Aylestone Park
NARBOROUGH ROAD ②
Former 6-car depot, closed 1922
Raw Dykes Road
River Soar
Duncan Road
Middleton St
Wigston Lane
AYLESTONE ROAD
AYLESTONE ⑤
NARBOROUGH RD.
to Hth St
Harlax
Narborough Road

1 mile
¾
½
¼
0
1000yards
1 kilometre
500
0.5
0

Central Area

Wharf St.
STREET Street
GATE
Belgrave Gate until 1930
O.S.
Charles St.
Bread St.
Depot
GALLOWTREE GATE HUMBERSTONE
Orchard St.
Lee Rd (Ubique)
BEDFORD STREET
Abbey St.
BELGRAVE GATE
HAY- MARKET
CLOCK TOWER
BOWLING GREEN ST.
Market Place
GRANBY ST.
BELVOIR ST.
POCKLING- TON'S WALK
LAYTON'S WALK
WELFORD ROAD
Burleys Lane
CHURCH GATE
East Bond St.
Gallowtree Gate
Cank St.
Silver St.
SANVEY GATE
Burgess St.
Grape St.
HIGH Southgate
Friar Lane
Millstone Lane
Newarke St.
Oxford St.
High Cross St.
GREAT CENTRAL STREET
ST NICHOLAS ST.
APPLE- GATE
BRIDGE ST.
Castle St.
The Newarke
NORTH GATE ST.
NGS
GCS
Original layout removed ca.1924
Central Station
Original layout
KING RICHARD'S ROAD
AUGUSTINE ST.
WEST BRIDGE ST.
BRAUN- STONE GATE
DUNN'S LANE
River Soar

Single as far as Bread St. until 1930.
HUMBERSTONE GATE
GALLOWTREE GATE
HAYMARKET
CHURCH GATE
Never used and all removed in 1924
EAST GATES
Cheapside
HIGH ST.
Silver St.
CLOCK TOWER 1904
300

CLOCK TOWER 1947 to 1949

Access faced east until 1922
HUMBERSTONE GATE
Central Depot
0   100   200 feet

Crossover installed 1906
CLOCK TOWER until 1947

Revised Routes 1948
BELGRAVE ①
MELTON ROAD ②
HUMBERSTONE ⑧
Coleman Road
EAST PARK ROAD
STONEYGATE ③
CLARENDON PARK ④
GROBY ROAD ⑨
Western Park
Narborough Road
Aylestone

Based on by J.C.Gillham's Map No. 85 (after K.W.Smith) dated August 1950, as revised (after M.S.W.Pearson) June 1970.
Drawn by R.A.Smith, January 2007. No. 770.

Uppingham Road was clear of traffic when No 140 was working on the East Park Circle.
(Albion Real Photo Series courtesy National Tramway Museum

The Melton Road service was discontinued on 3 July 1949 and the Belgrave route was linked to Stoneygate, service 3. No 129 is at Melton Road junction on 29 July 1949. (R.J.S.Wiseman

At least one centre bracket-arm pole still remained in the city when No 119 was photographed on East Park Road on 28 February 1948. (R.J.S.Wiseman

A row of shops was often a feature of suburban tram termini. No 154 was photographed at Aylestone terminus in 1938. *(W.A. Camwell, National Tramway Museum*

No 169 en-route along the London Road to Stoneygate takes up passengers from the loading island outside London Road L.M.S. Station on 25 May 1938. *(H.B.Priestley, National Tramway Museum*

Nos 101 and 131 at Western Park terminus on 21 November 1948 the last day the services to Western Park and Narborough operated. Did it always rain when lines closed in Leicester? It also rained on the final day in 1949!   *(W.A. Camwell,courtesy National Tramway Museum*

It was also raining on 7 May 1938 when Nos. 19 and 158 were photographed at Narborough terminus.
(W.A. Camwell, courtesy National Tramway Museum

London Road was deserted on Saturday 11 June 1949 when two passengers waited to board No 72 at the Toller Road stop. *(R.J.S.Wiseman*

Withdrawn trams were lined up on a siding at the Abbey Park Road depot. On 5 February 1949 Nos 120, 144 and at least two others were awaiting their fate. *(R.J.S.Wiseman*

Newark on Trent

The direct route to Newark is to follow the Fosse Way northwards for 33 miles, but it is still possible to travel by the old Midland Railway via Nottingham. Newark is a small market town with a XIIth century castle. where the Newark and District Light Railway Company, a subsidiary of the Notts & Derby Tramway Company, was authorised by the Newark and District Light Railway Order 1906 to build 3½ miles of 4ft 8½in. gauge electric tramway, although these powers eventually lapsed. The trams would have run from the Great Northern station through the town centre and along the Fosse Way to Farndon or south along the Great North Road to Balderton.

Lincoln

Following the Fosse Way for a further 16 miles or continuing on the Midland Railway, we come to the cathedral city of Lincoln sited in the gap of the Lincoln Edge formed by the River Witham. The Lincoln Tramway Company introduced horse trams on 8 September 1882 from the High Bridge on the edge of the old city along the valley of the Witham to Bracebridge, a distance of 1¾ miles. The track gauge was 3ft. 6in. and the line was worked by ten single-deck tramcars. various extensions were considered, but no further lines were built.

Electrification was considered as early as 1899 for routes involving steep gradients to serve older parts of the city, but no progress was made at this time. Five years later, after much discussion the tramway company was purchased by the corporation which had resolved to convert the line to electric traction using the Griffiths-Bedell surface-contact system.

The line was rebuilt to standard gauge and reopened on 23 November 1905 with a mixture of open-top and balcony cars. The surface contact system with its metal studs was not really successful and the line converted to overhead wire from the end of 1919. The authorised extensions to Monks Road and elsewhere were not built, and the line closed on 4 March 1929.

Lincolnshire

Several rural steam tramways were planned in various parts of Lincolnshire. From Lincoln itself the Brigg Tramway Company was authorised in 1881 to build 23 miles of 3ft.6in. gauge track northwards to Brigg, a small market town, but although some track was laid near Hibaldstow. south of Brigg, the line was never completed or opened. Further east, the Alford and Sutton Tramway Company, later the Great Northern Steam Tramways Co. Ltd., opened a seven mile 2ft. 6in. steam line from Alford to Sutton-on-Sea from 1884, until a full-size railway reached Sutton by a different route in 1889. Another 2ft. 6in. gauge 13½ mile line was authorised in 1883 to the Skegness, Chapel St. Leonards and Alford Tramway, but it was never built, nor was the twelve mile standard gauge line from Boston to Wrangle, authorised in 1878 to the Boston District Tramways Company, which had applied in 1877 for a six mile line from Wrangle to Wainfleet.

Finally, to conclude this survey, according to a local history book, a horse tramway was operated for a time at Skegness after the promenade had been built in 1879.

It was built about 1880 and ran for two or three summer seasons. It was a quarter of a mile in length and ran out onto the beach. It had two one-horse cross bench cars with canvas sunshade roofs.

All the trams owned by the Lincoln Tramways Company were suited for one-horse operation. This is one of the Ashbury cars at the city terminus. (Courtesy National Tramway Museum

There was a trial run with No 6 on 11 November 1905 and the scene is at Bracebridge, probably outside the depot. Note the gentleman with the brush, did he clean malfunctioning studs?
(Courtesy National Tramway Museum

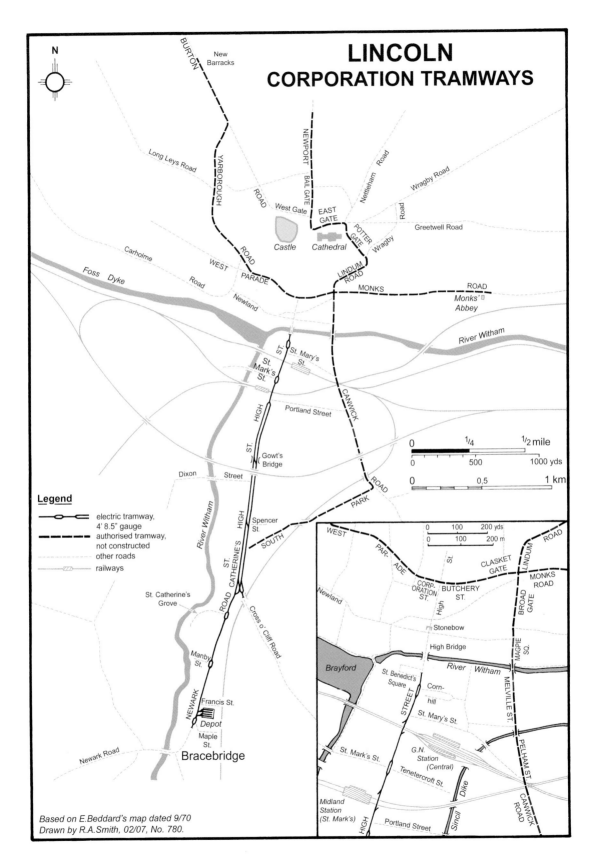

LINCOLN
CORPORATION TRAMWAYS

N

New Barracks
BURTON
Long Leys Road
NEWPORT
YARBOROUGH ROAD
BAIL GATE
Nettleham Road
Wragby Road
West Gate
EAST GATE
Road
Greetwell Road
POTTER GATE
Wragby
Castle
Cathedral
WEST PARADE
Carholme
Road
LINDUM ROAD
MONKS ROAD
Foss Dyke
Newland
Monks' Abbey
River Witham
St. Mary's St.
ST
St. Mark's St.
HIGH ST.
Portland Street
CANWICK
Gowt's Bridge
Dixon Street
ROAD
River Witham
HIGH ST.
Spencer St.
PARK
SOUTH
ROAD CATHERINE'S ST.
Cross o' Cliff Road
St. Catherine's Grove
Manby St.
NEWARK
Francis St.
Depot
Maple St.
Newark Road
Bracebridge

0   ¼   ½ mile
0   500   1000 yds
0   0,5   1 km

Legend
⊶⊶ electric tramway, 4' 8.5" gauge
▬ ▬ authorised tramway, not constructed
- - - other roads
▭ railways

WEST PAR-ADE
St.
CLASKET GATE
LINDUM ROAD
CORP-ORATION ST.
BUTCHERY ST.
MONKS ROAD
Newland
High
BROAD GATE
MAGPIE SQ.
Stonebow
High Bridge
MELVILLE ST.
Brayford
St. Benedict's Square
River Witham
Corn-hill
St. Mary's St.
STREET
PELHAM ST.
St. Mark's St.
G.N. Station (Central)
HIGH
Tenetercroft St.
Sincil Dike
CANWICK ROAD
Midland Station (St. Mark's)
Portland Street

0   100   200 yds
0   100   200 m

Based on E.Beddard's map dated 9/70
Drawn by R.A.Smith, 02/07, No. 780.

Nos 2 and 3 were never top-covered. No 3 stands at Bracebridge terminus on Saturday 2 March 1929 two days before the last car, No 6 ran back to the depot. *(Dr H. Nicol National Tramway Museum*

Lincoln High Street viewed from the Great Northern Railway level crossing with the catch points in the foreground. The Great Northern Hotel featured in the 1922 Michelin Guide while the signal on the right in front of St. Mary-le-Wilford's Chapel indicates the road is clear.

(F.Frith & Co. Ltd. Courtesy National Tramway Museum

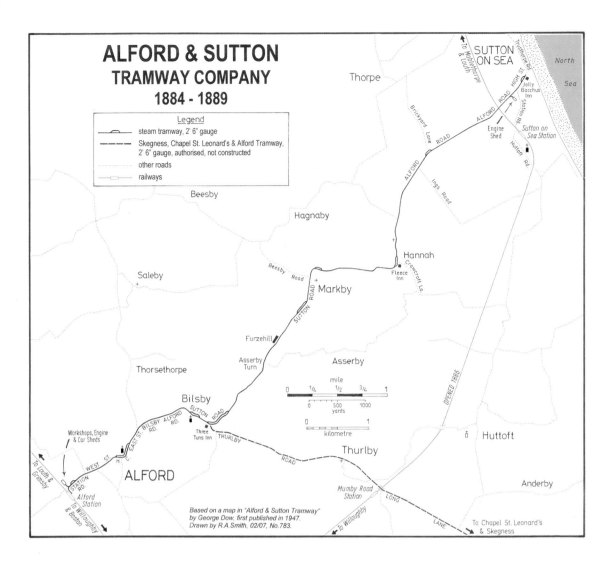

ALFORD & SUTTON
TRAMWAY COMPANY
1884 - 1889

Legend
- steam tramway, 2' 6" gauge
- Skegness, Chapel St. Leonard's & Alford Tramway, 2' 6" gauge, authorised, not constructed
- other roads
- railways

SUTTON ON SEA

North Sea

Thorpe

Beesby

Hagnaby

Saleby

Markby

Hannah

Fleece Inn

Furzehill

Asserby Turn

Asserby

Thorsethorpe

Bilsby

Three Tuns Inn

Workshops, Engine & Car Sheds

ALFORD

Alford Station

To Louth & Grimsby

To Willoughby & Boston

Thurlby

Huttoft

Anderby

Mumby Road Station

To Willoughby

To Chapel St. Leonard's & Skegness

Engine Shed

Sutton on Sea Station

Jolly Bacchus Inn

To Mablethorpe & Louth

Based on a map in "Alford & Sutton Tramway" by George Dow, first published in 1947. Drawn by R.A.Smith, 02/07, No.783.

OPENED 1886

Locomotive No. 2 with a wagon and single-truck trailer.
(Merryweather & Sons, National Tramway Museum

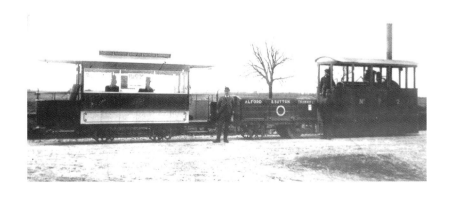

Locomotive No. 2 the eight-wheel trailer and one of the four-wheelers posed for the camera.
(National Tramway Museum

Most of the population of Alford appear to have witnessed the opening of the line on 2 April 1884.
(National Tramway Museum

Tramcar Fleet Lists

All cars were four-wheel double-deck unless otherwise stated.

Seating figures are shown 22/34 for lower saloon and upper deck respectively.

The opening dates shown are the first day of public service.

The closing dates shown for horse operation are the day the service closed usually under another operator.; for electric services it is the last day of full public service.

Alford and Sutton Tramway

7.00 Miles, 2ft.6in. gauge. Steam traction.

Opened 2 April 1884, closed December 1889. Livery:,Locomotives believed to be yellow or red and yellow.

Trailers pale yellow or cream

Locomotives	No 1 Black Hawthorne (Wilkinson Patent), 1883
	No 2 Merryweather, 1883.
	No 3 Dick Kerr, 1885
Trailers	Four single-deck, four-wheel
	One single-deck eight-wheel

Ashover Light Railway

7.15 miles, 2ft.0in gauge, steam operated.

Opened 7 April 1925,

Closed to passenger service 13 September 1936, mineral service 31 March 1950.

Rolling stock: 6 040T locomotives, 4 saloon coaches, 8 open coaches and 70 mineral wagons.

Burton-on-Trent Corporation Tramways

6.66 miles, 3ft.6in. gauge. Opened 3 August 1903, closed 31 December 1929.

Livery crimson lake and cream.

Car Number	Type (as built)	Year Built	Builder	Seats	Trucks	Motors	Controllers
1 - 20 (a)	Open top	1903	ER & TCW	22/21	Brill 21E	DK25 2 x 25hp	DK DB1 Form C
21 - 24 (b)	Balcony	1920	EE	22/24	Preston 21E	DK29 2 x 30hp	DK DB1 K3

Notes : Eight cars were hired from Great Yarmouth Corporation from September 1918 until March 1919, but believed not to have run in Burton.

(a)   Nos.7,8,9,10,11,17 received balcony top covers; 3 by Milnes Voss in 1904; 3 by UEC 1906.

(b)   Sold to York in 1930, converted open top, numbered 42-45.

Burton & Ashby Light Railway

10 miles, 3ft,6in. gauge. Opened 13 June 1906, closed 19 February 1927.
Livery crimson lake, from 1920 maroon and white.

Car Number	Type (as built)	Year Built	Builder	Seats	Trucks	Motors	Controllers
1 - 13	Open top	1905	Brush	22/31	Brush AA	Westinghouse 2 x 25hp	Westinghouse 210
14 - 20	Open top	1906	Brush	22/31	Brush AA	Westinghouse 2 x 25hp	Westinghouse 210

On closure ten cars were sold to Tynemouth and District, their numbers 22-31. Some motors sold to Salford. No.14 preserved.

Chesterfield and District Tramways Company Ltd.

1.3 miles, 4ft. 8½ in. gauge. Horse traction. Opened 8 November 1882, succeeded by the Chesterfield Tramways Company in December 1886 and passed to the Corporation on 22 November 1897 and closed late in 1904.
Livery Prussian blue and primrose.
Rolling stock - Nos.1-2 double-deck, No.3 single-deck all by Ashbury 1882.
Nos.4,5 single-deck, probably by Milnes. Under Corporation ownership Nos.6-8, single-deck seating 16 by Milnes..No.8 preserved at Crich.

Chesterfield Corporation Tramways

3.62 miles, 4ft.8 in. Opened 23 December1904, closed 23 May 1927.
Replaced by trolleybuses which ran until 24 March 1938.

Car Number	Type (as built)	Year Built	Builder	Seats	Trucks	Motors	Controllers
1 - 12 (a)	Open top	1904	Brush	22/34	Brush Conaty	Westinghouse 2 x 25hp	Westinghouse 90
13 - 14 (b)	Open top	1907	Brush	22/34	Brush Special	Westinghouse 2 x 25hp	Westinghouse 90
15	Water car Single-deck	1909	Brush		Brush Special	Westinghouse 2 x 25hp	Westinghouse 90M
16 - 18 (c)	Balcony	1914	Brush	22/24	Peckham P22	Westinghouse 2 x 25hp	Westinghouse 90

Notes.
(a)   No.8 was destroyed by fire in 1916 and replaced in 1920.
      Nos.6,7,8,9,11,12 received balcony top covers in 1919-1920.
      No.7 restored and now at Crich.
(b)   No.14 balcony top cover 1920.
(c)   One of these cars, was also destroyed by fire in 1916 and replaced in 1920.

Crich. National Tramway Museum.

1.00 miles, 4ft.8½ in. Opened horse traction 2 June 1963, electric 5 July 1964. Livery as when in corporation or company service.

Car Number	Type (as built)	Year Built	Original Owner	Notes	
1	Open top	1904	Derby Corporation	Display	(a)
1	Open top	1896	Douglas Southern	Display	(b)
1	Enclosed	1932	London County Council	Display	(c)
1	Open top	1881	Leamington & Warwick	Display	Horse tram
2	Toastrack	1898	Blackpool Corporation		
4	Open top	1885	Blackpool Corporation	Display	
5	Single-deck	1927	Gateshead and District		
7	Open top	1904	Chesterfield Corporation		(d)
8	Single-deck	1899	Chesterfield Corporation	Horse tram	(e)
9	Single-deck	1873	Porto Municipal Transport.	Horse tram.	
10	Open top	1902	Hill of Howth GNR(I)		
14	Single-deck	1915	Great Central Railway, Grimsby & Immingham Line.		
15	Single-deck	1874	Sheffield Tramways Company	Horse tram,	
21	Enclosed	1894	Dundee and District	Display	(f)
22	Balcony	1922	Glasgow Corporation		
35	Enclosed	1048	City & Royal Burgh of Edinburgh	Display	(g)
40	Balcony	1926	Blackpool Corporation		
40	Single-deck	1914	Blackpool and Fleetwood Company.		
45	Open top	1903	Southampton Corporation		
46	Single-deck	1899	Sheffield Corporation	In store.	(h)
49	Enclosed	1926	Blackpool Corporation		
52	Single-deck	1920	Gateshead and District Tramways Co,		
59	Open top	1903	Blackpool Corporation	Dreadnought	In store
60	Balcony	1906	Johannesburg Corporation		
68	Open top	1919	Paisley District Tramways		
74	Open platform	1900	Sheffield Corporation		(i)
76	Balcony	1904	Leicester Corporation	Display	(j)
92	Lower Saloon	1923	Nottingham Corporation		(k)
102	Open top	1902	Newcastle Corporation.		
106	Open top	1903	London County Council		(l)
132	Enclosed	1910	Hull Corporation.	At Hull Museum.	
159	Open top	1903	London United Tramways		(m)
166	Lower Saloon	1920	Nottingham Corporation		(n)
166	Open toastrack	1927	Blackpool Corporation		
167	Single-deck	1928	Blackpool Corporation	'Pantograph'	
180	Enclosed	1931	Leeds Corporation	'Horsfield'	
180	Single-deck	1905	Prague City Tramways		
189	Enclosed	1934	Sheffield Corporation		
264	Enclosed	1937	Sheffield Corporation		
273	Single-deck	1927	Porto City Tramways		(o)
298	Railcoach	1933	Blackpool Corporation		(p)
331	Enclosed	1930	Metropolitan Tramways	'Feltham'	(q)
345	Enclosed	1912	Leeds Corporation		
399	Enclosed	1925	Leeds Corporation		
510	Enclosed	1950	Sheffield Corporation		
600	Single-deck	1954	Leeds Corporation	In store	(r)

Crich. National Tramway Museum.(continued)

Car Number	Type (as built)	Year Built	Original Owner	Notes	
602	Railcoach	1953	Leeds Corporation		
674	Single-deck	1939	New York Third Avenue Transit		(s)
765	Single-deck	1914	Manchester Corporation		(t)
802	Single-deck	1960	Halle City Tramways	Access Car	
812	Enclosed	1900	Glasgow Corporation		
869	Enclosed	1936	Liverpool Corporation		
1100	Enclosed	1928	Glasgow Corporation	In store	
1115	Enclosed	1929	Glasgow Corporation		
1147	Single-deck	1960	The Hague City Tramways	PCC Car	Display.
1282	Enclosed	1940	Glasgow Corporation	'Coronation'	
1297	Enclosed	1948	Glasgow Corporation	'Cunarder'	
1622	Enclosed	1912	London County Council		(u)
2006	Single-deck	1969	Berlin City Tramways	Access car.	
	Steam Tram	1885	Beyer Peacock		(v)
	Horse tram	1895	London Tramways Company		(w)

Works Cars

Car Number	Type (as built)	Year Built	Original Owner	Notes	
1	Mains Car	1905	Glasgow Corporation		
2	Railgrinder	1928	Blackpool Corporation	In store	
2	Tower Car	1932	Leeds Corporation.		
21	Tool Van	1903	Glasgow Corporation		
65	Coal Carrier	19—	Porto Municipal Transport	In store.	
86	Snowbroom	19—	Brussels City Tramways.		
131	Water Car	1905	Cardiff Corporation		(x)
330	Water Car	1919	Sheffield Corporation	Ex-Bradford No.251.	
Loco	Steeple-cab	1927	Blackpool Corporation		

Notes

(a) Restored 1962-92 to 1928 condition with balcony top-cover.
(b) Property of Science Museum
(c) Leeds 301, 1951-59.
(d) Restored 1995-97 to 1920 condition with balcony top-cover.
(e) Restored by Chesterfield Corporation. Owned by National Museum of Science and Technology.
(f) Steam tram trailer, Restored 1993-95.
(g) On loan from City and Royal Burgh of Edinburgh.
(h) Restored at Sheffield after serving as a snowplough.
(i) Restored 1993-95.
(j) Restored 1973-75.
(k) To be displayed in pre-restored condition.
(l) Restored 1971-83 by LCC Tramways Trust.
(m) Being restored 2007.
(n) To be restored to double-deck condition.
(o) Restored 1999-01.
(p) Restored 2007.
(q) Sunderland 100 1937-52
(r) Ex-Sunderland 85
(s) Wien (Vienna) 4225 1948-90.
(t) Restored in 1977, At Heaton Park, Manchester.
(u) Restored by LCC Tramways Trust 1984-94.
(v) Worked in Sydney, Australia 1855-90.
(w) Known as the Curry Rivel tram from where it was rescued in 1984.
(x) The first tram to arrive at Crich in May 1959.

The four-mile Douglas Southern Tramway along the Marine Drive on the Isle of Man had a fleet of 8 open-top tramcars built in 1896. No 1 was rescued in 1951 and after a time at the Clapham Museum came to Crich in 1975. It is seen outside the exhibition hall on 29 August 1998.

(R.J.S. Wiseman

Gateshead No.5 at the Town End terminus at Crich on 16 June 2002.   *(R.J.S. Wiseman*

Derby Tramways Company Ltd.

4.68 miles, 4ft.0in. gauge. Opened 1880, closed 28 November 1907.
23 double-deck cars, livery crimson lake or scarlet and offwhite.

Derby Corporation Tramways

13.96 miles, 4ft.0in. gauge. Opened 27 July 1904, closed 2 July 1934.
Livery olive green and cream. The trams were replaced by trolleybuses which ran from 9 January 1932 to 9 September 1967.

Car Number	Type (as built)	Year Built	Builder	Seats	Trucks	Motors	Controllers
1 - 25 (a)	Open top	1904	Brush	22/26	Brush AA	BTH GE52 2 x 25hp	GE K10
26 - 29 (b)	Balcony	1905	Brush	22/26	Brush Conaty	BTH GE52 2 x 25hp	GE K10
30 - 35 (b)	Balcony	1906	Milnes Voss	22/30	M&G Radial	BTH GE52 2 x 25hp	GE K10
36 - 39 (c)	Single-deck	1906	Milnes Voss	32	M&G	BTH GE52 Radial	GE K10 2 x 25hp
40 - 41 (d)	Open top	1907	Milnes Voss	18/24	M&G 21EM	BTH GE52 2 x 25hp	GE K10
42 - 44 (b,d)	Open top	1907	Milnes Voss	22/30	M&G Radial	BTH GE54 2 x 25hp	GE K10
45 - 47 (e)	Open top	1908	Milnes Voss	22/30	M&G 21EM	BTH GE54 2 x 25hp	GE K10
48 - 50	Balcony	1911	Brush	22/30	Brush Flexible	BTH GE200 2 x 30hp	GE K10
51 - 60 (f)	Balcony	1920-1	Brush	22/30	Peckham P22	BTH GE200 2 x 30hp	GE K10
61 - 78 (f)	Enclosed	1925-8	Brush	22/30	Peckham P22	BTH GE200 2 x 30hp	BTH B510

Notes
(a) All, except 12,15,18 fitted Brill 21E trucks. No.1 preserved at Crich.
  Nos. 1,3,4,8,9,22,23 rebuilt with new Brush top-covers between 1923-1927
  No 5 became a works car
(b) Trucks replaced by Peckham P21B in 1913, by Peckham P22 in 1920-21.
(c) When the railway bridge in Friargate was reconstructed to allow double- deck cars through, these cars were relegated to workmens specials.
(d) Fitted top covers in 1913-14.
(e) One car fitted GE 200 motors, also as notes b,d.
(f) All originally fitted with GE K10 controllers. 18 cars,, presumably, 61-78 fitted B510 controllers.

Ilkeston Corporation Tramways

3.78 miles, 3ft. 6in. gauge. Opened 16 May 1903,
Operation taken over by the Notts & Derby Company on 16 November 1916 and purchased in 1922.
Closed 6 February 1931. Trolleybuses operated from 7 January 1932 until 25 April 1953.

Car Number	Type (as built)	Year Built	Builder	Seats	Trucks	Motors	Controllers
1 - 9	Open top	1902	ER&TCW	22/26	Brill 21E	DK25B 2 x 25hp	DK DB1 Form B
10 -13	Open top	1903	Milnes	22/26	Brill 21E	Westinghouse 46M 2 x 25hp	Westinghouse 210

Notes   Eight cars were rebuilt by Notts & Derby at Langley Mill. No.7 was converted to one-man single-deck for the Ilkeston Junction service.
Two cars transferred to Dunfermline, Nos.44-45, and three to Carlisle Nos.13-15(ii), also Balfour Beatty owned.

Leicester Tramways Company Ltd.

9.00 miles, 4ft.8½ in. gauge. Horse traction. Opened 24 December 1874, closed October 1904. Livery grey and biscuit. Rolling stock 46 double-deck and single-deck cars. A Hughes Patent steam tram operated for some time in 1878 before transfer to Govan, Glasgow.

Three single deck tramcars, Nos. 36-39, were supplied by Milnes Voss in 1906 for service on the Ashbourne Road.   *(Courtesy National Tramway Museum*

Leicester Corporation Tramways

22.95 miles, 4ft.8¹/₂ in. gauge. Opened 18 May 1904, closed 9 November 1949.
Livery Maroon and cream.

Car Number	Type (as built)	Year Built	Builder	Seats	Trucks	Motors	Controllers
1 - 99 (a)	Open top	1904	ER&TCW	22/34	Brill 21E	DK 25A 2 x 25hp	DK DB1 Form B
100 (b)	Water car	1904	ER&TCW	-	Brill	21E DK 25A 2 x 25hp	DK DB1 Form B
101 - 121 (c)	Balcony	1905	UEC	22/34	Brill	21E DK 3A4 2 X 35hp	DK DB1 Form G
122 - 141 (d)	Open top	1905	UEC	22/34	Brill	21E DK 3A4 2 x 35hp	DK DB1 Form G
142 (e)	Water car	1905	UEC	-	Brill 21E	DK 25A 2 x 25hp	DK DB1 Form B
143 (e)	Water car	1909	UEC	-	Brill 21E	DK 3A4 2 x 35hp	DK DB1 Form G
141-143 (ii) 144-150 (f)	Balcony	1913	UEC	22/38	Brill 21E	DK 20A 2 x 40hp	DK DB1 K3
151-153 (ii) 154-160 (g)	Balcony	1914	Brush	22/38	Brill 21E	DK 20A 2 x 40hp	DK DB1 K3
161 - 166 (g)	Balcony	1920	LCT	22/34	Preston 21E	DK20A 2 x 40hp	DK DB1 K3
167 - 178 (g)	Balcony	1920	EE	22/34	Preston 21E	DK 20A 2 x 40hp	DK DB1 K3

Notes	A sample car was obtained from Brush in 1903 and resold to Metropolitan Electric Tramways.
	Cars with 25hp motors were re-equipped with 45hp motors of types DK 30, DK 108, BTH 502, or BTH 265, and in some cases with new BTH or MV controllers.
(a	No.1 was delivered in 1903. All fitted balcony covers 1912-27, and all, except Nos.12,24,29,44, fully enclosed 1924-37 .
(b)	Renumbered 151 in 1912 and 179 in 1920.
(c)	Fully enclosed 1924-1934
(d	In 1912 No.137 renumbered 100 and No.141 renumbered 137. All except 122 and 128 enclosed as note a.
(e)	Nos.142-143 were renumbered 152-153 in 1912 and 180-181 in 1920.
(f)	PAYE cars when first in service. Fully enclosed 1924-1934.

Lincoln Tramway Company Ltd.

1.75 miles, 3ft.6in. gauge. Horse traction. Opened 8 September 1882, closed 22 July 1905. Livery red and cream or brown and cream.

Rolling stock, all single-deck; Nos.1-3 1882-3 Ashbury, 16 seats; Nos. 4-6 1883-5 Ashbury, 22 seats; Nos.7-8 1899 own build, 32 seats, possibly secondhand from Gravesend. Nos.9-10 1900 Falcon, 18 seats.

City of Lincoln Tramways

1.75 miles, 4ft.8½ in.gauge. Opened 23 November 1905, closed 4 March 1929.
Livery light green and white.

Car Number	Type (as built)	Year Built	Builder	Seats	Trucks	Motors	Controllers
1 - 6 (a)	Open top	1905	Brush	22/30	Brush Conaty	Westinghouse 2 x 25hp	Westinghouse
7 - 8	Balcony	1905	Brush	22/30	Brush Conaty	Westinghouse 2 x 35hp	Westinghouse
9 - 11 (b)	Balcony	1919	EE	22/30	Preston 21E	DK 30B 2 x 40hp	DK DB1 K4
32 - 33 (c)	Open top	Bought 1918	-	?	Trunnions	-	-

Notes

The Griffiths-Bedall surface-contact system was used until December 1919.

(a)   Nos.1,4,5,6 received Milnes Voss top covers, 2 cars in 1907, 2 cars in 1908. No.6 was totally enclosed in 1924.

(b)   Nos. 9-11 were sold to Preston in 1929, their numbers 13,18,22.

(c)   Horse tram trailers bought from Great Grimsby Street Tramways. Probably originally numbered 11 and 14. Ran until 1921

No 9 at Bracebridge, was new in 1919 from English Electric at Preston, and after the Lincoln system closed saw further service in the town of its birth.

(Dr H. Nicol, National Tramway Museum

Mansfield & District Light Railway Company.

12,25 miles,4ft.8$\frac{1}{2}$ in. gauge. Opened 11 July 1905, closed 9 October 1932.
Livery originally post office red and cream,later light green and cream..

Car Number	Type (as built)	Year Built	Builder	Seats	Trucks	Motors	Controllers
1 - 12 (a)	Open top	1905	Hurst Nelson	22/25	HN 21E	Westinghouse 200 2 x 25hp	Westinghouse 90
13 - 18 (a)	Balcony	1906	Brush	22/25	Brush AA	Westinghouse 200 2 x 25hp	Westinghouse 90
19 - 20 (b)	Open top	1906	Brush	72	Brush Conaty	BTH 2 x 25hp	BTH B18?
-	Water car	1906	Brush	-	Brush	Westinghouse 2 x 25hp	? ?
21 - 22 (c)	Balcony	1911	UEC	22/34	Peckham P22	BTH GE67 2 x 40hp	GE K10D
23 -24 (c)	Open top	1912	UEC	22/34	Peckham P22	BTH GE67 2 x 40hp	GE K10D
25 - 28 (d	Balcony	1916	UEC	22/34	Peckham P22	BTH GE67 2 x 40hp	GE K10D
27 - 28 (ii) (e)	Enclosed	1925	EE	26/40	Peckham P22	BTH 506A 2 x 40hp	BTH 510A
29 - 31 (f)	Open top	1913	UEC	24/32	Peckham P22	BTH GE20 3N 2 x 40hp	GE K10D
29(ii) (g)	Balcony	1913	UEC	24/32	Peckham P22	BTH GE20 3N 2 x 40hp	GE K10D

Notes
(a) Nos. 1,4,9,11 were fitted balcony top covers and No.5 extensively rebuilt c1926. Nos.5,13,19,20 later fitted Peckham P22 trucks.
  On some cars Westinghouse 90 controllers were replaced by Westinghouse T2A or BTH B18.
(b) Ex-Cavehill & Whitewell purchased 1912 Later fitted Peckham P22 trucks.
(c) Total seating 56, lower saloon probably 22.
  Nos.23-24 were sold to Llanelly, an associated company, in 1918, .
  Believed their numbers 16,17.
(d) Nos.27,28 renumbered 23,24 after the sale to Llanelly.
(e) Sold to Sunderland Corporation after closure, their Nos.21,24..
(f) Loaned from Notts & Derby Company in 1925, No.29 returned after a year.
(g)   Loaned from Notts & Derby in 1929 to replace No.26 damaged in an accident.

Matlock Cable Tramway Company Ltd.

0.62 miles, 3ft.6in. gauge. Cable, maximum gradient 1 in 5. Opened 28 March 1893.
Gifted to the Urban District Council in 1898. Closed 30 September 1927.
Three open top bogie cars by Milnes seating 13/18.
Livery royal blue and white.

Nottinghamshire & Derbyshire Tramways Company

11.37 miles, 4ft.8½ in. gauge. Opened 4 July 1913 and through to Nottingham on 15 January 1914. closed, regular service 30 December 1931, peak hours services or at least one car per day until 4 October 1932. The trams were replaced by trolleybuses which ran via Nottingham Road and Mansfield Road to King Street, Queen Street, Nottingham, until 25 April 1953.

Car Number	Type (as built)	Year Built	Builder	Seats	Trucks	Motors	Controllers
1 - 12 (a)	Open top	1913	UEC	24/32	Peckham P22	BTH GE203N 2 x 40hp	GE K1 10D
13 - 24 (b)	Balcony	1913	UEC	24/32	Peckham P22	BTH GE 203N 2 x 40hp	GE K1 10D

Notes.
a)   Nos.1-3 were fitted with EE balcony covers in 1922. Three cars were loaned to Mansfield in 1925. One was returned after a few months.
b)   One car was loaned to Mansfield in 1929.

Nottingham and District Tramways Company Ltd.

7.50 miles, 4ft.8½ in. gauge. Horse and steam traction. Opened 17 September 1878, closed 30 April 1902. Livery according to route, Yellow Trent Bridge, Red Carrington, Dark Blue Basford.
Rolling stock.
Single-deck horse trams
Nos.1-8 Starbuck 1878, No.12 Stevenson 1879,
Nos.13-24 Starbuck 1880-83, No.19 rebuilt double-deck 1885.
Nos.25,26, summer cars, Starbuck 1884. Nos.27-28 Starbuck, 1885.

Single-deck toastracks
Nos. 19(ii), 34(ii), later 35(ii), of 1891. Builders not known.

Double-deck horse trams (open top).
Nos.9-11 Stevenson 1879, . No.30 MC&T 1887. Nos.31-34 converted horse buses by Andrews of Carrington 1888 Nos.31,32 renumbered 35,36 in 1891.
Nos.31-34 Milnes 1891-2.
A steam tram engine inscribed 'Made in Wigan, 1882' was purchased in 1883. This ran with top covered bogie trailer No.29 seating 100 on the Basford route until 1889.
No.29 Starbuck 1885, rebuilt open top on single-truck 1889

Nottingham Corporation Tramways.

25.5 miles, 4ft 8½in gauge. Opened 1 January 1901, closed 5 September 1936. Livery maroon and cream. Most routes except the last replaced by trolleybuses which operated from 10 April 1927 until 1 July 1966.

Car Number	Type (as built)	Year Built	Builder	Seats	Trucks	Motors	Controllers
1 - 25 (a)	Open top	1900-1	ER&TCW	22/34	Brill 21E	DK 25A 2 x 25hp	DK DE1
26 - 57 (a)	Open top	1901	ER&TCW	22/34	Brill 21E	DK 35A 2 x 35hp	DK DE1 Form A
58- 67 (a,b)	Open top	1901	Milnes	22/34	Brill 21E	Westinghouse 2 x 30hp	BTH B18
68 - 77 (c)	Open top	1901	Milnes	30/40	Brill 22E bogies	Westinghouse 2 x 30hp	BTH GE K10?
78 - 83 (a)	Open top	1902	Milnes	22/34	Brill 21E	BTH GE58 2 x 37hp	BTH B18
84 - 89	Open top	1902	Milnes	30/40	Brill 22E bogies	BTH GE58 2 x 37hp	BTH GEK10
90- 105 (a)	Open top	1902	ER&TCW	22/34	Brill 21E	DK 3A3 2 x 35hp	DK DE1 Form B
106 - 115 (d)	Balcony	1907	Milnes Voss	22/34	M&G 21EM	DK3A4 2 x 35hp	DK DE1 Form B
116 - 125	Balcony	1908	UEC	22/34	Brill 21E	DK 3A4 2 x 35hp	DK DB1 K3
126 - 135 (e)	Balcony	1912	UEC	22/38	Brill 21E	DK 9A2 2 x 40hp	DK DB1 K3
136 - 145	Balcony	1914	UEC	22/42	Preston Flexible	DK 9A3 2 x 40hp	DK DB1 K3
146 - 155	Balcony	1914	Brush	22/42	Peckham P22	DK 9A3 2 x 40hp	DK DB1 K3
156 - 180	Balcony	1920	EE	22/42	Preston Flexible	DK30B 2 x 40hp	DK DB1 K3
181 - 200 (f)	Enclosed	1926-7	EE	24/46	Peckham P22	DK 30B 2 x 40hp	DK DB1 K3
1	Water Car	1901	ER&TCW	-	Brill 21E	DK 25A	DK
2	Snowplough	1901	R&TCW	-	Brill 21E	DK 25A	DK

Nottingham Corporation Tramways. contd

Notes   Between 1914 and 1924 Brush and UEC later EE supplied 67 lower saloons to replace those of most single-truck cars built up to 1902. These cars were also re-equipped with DK9A or DK30B 40hp motors and DB1 K3 controllers

(a)   Balcony top covers fitted between 1904 and 1914. Nos. 33, 82 initially fitted Bellamy covers in 1904.

(b)   Ordered from British Electric Car Company who subcontracted to Milnes

(c)   Retrucked with Brill 27G bogies and fitted with four motors in 1902. Balcony covers

(d)   Most rebuilt with new EE lower saloons and Brill 21E trucks.

(e)   Preston semi-convertible cars.

(f)   All except No. 195 sold to Aberdeen Corporation. Their Nos. 1-18 (ii).

(g)   Fully enclosed 1924-1934.

Nottingham Express Transit

8.70 miles, 14kms, 4ft 8½in. gauge. Opened 9 March 2004. Livery dark green, silver and white.

Car Number	Type (as built)	Year Built	Builder	Seats	Trucks	Motors	Controllers
201 - 215	Incentro Single-deck low floor	2003	Bombardier	64	Three axleless bogies	Eight water cooled	2 x GBT

The trams, the first low-floor in UK have five-section articulated bodies and space for further 130 standing passengers. Based on a similar design in use in Nantes.

On 1 May 2005 No. 203 arrives at the Forest to pick up passengers who will have left their cars at this large Park & Ride site.   *(R.J.S. Wiseman*

Key to Abbreviations and Manufacturers

Ashbury	The Ashbury Railway Carriage and Iron Co. Ltd. Manchester.
BEC	The British Electric Car Co. Ltd.,Trafford Park, Manchester.
Bombardier	Bombardier Ltd., Derby.
Brill	The J.G.Brill Company, Philadelphia, USA.
Brush	The Brush Electrical Engineering Co. Ltd., Loughborough.
BTH	British Thomson-Houston Company Ltd.
Conaty	Conaty & Lycett Radial trucks made by Brush.
DK	Dick Kerr & Co. Ltd., Preston.
EE	English Electric Company Ltd. Preston
Falcon	Falcon Engine and Car Works Ltd., Loughborough.
ER&TCW	The Electric Railway & Tramway Carriage Works Ltd., Preston.
GE	The General Electric Company, Schenectady, USA.
Griffiths-Bedell	Griffiths-Bedell Company Ltd., Ilford
Hughes	Henry Hughes & Co. Falcon Works, Loughborough.
LCT	Leicester Corporation Tramways
MC&T	The Manchester Carriage & Tramways Company, Pendleton Works
Milnes	Geo. F. Milnes & Co. Ltd., Hadley, Shropshire, also Birkenhead
Milnes Voss	G.C.Milnes, Voss & Co. Ltd., Birkenhead.
M & G	Mountain & Gibson Ltd., Bury, Lancashire.
MV	The Metropolitan Vickers Electrical Co. Ltd., Trafford Park, Manchester.
PAYE	Pay as you enter system of fare collection.
Peckham	Peckham Truck & Engineering Co. Ltd.
Preston 21E	Preston 21E type trucks manufactured by Dick, Kerr & Co. Ltd.
Starbuck	Starbuck Car & Wagon Co. Ltd., Birkenhead
Stephenson	Stephenson Carriage & Wagon Co., New York, USA.
UEC	United Electric Car Company Ltd., Preston
Westinghouse	Westinghouse Electric Co. Ltd., Trafford Park, Manchester

The Electric Tramway & Carriage Works Ltd. (renamed United Electric Car Company Ltd., from 25 September 1905) was a subsidiary of Dick, Kerr & Co. Ltd which merged with other electrical companies on 14 December 1918 to form the English Electric Company Ltd.

Most post 1908 Peckham trucks were made by the Brush Electrical Engineering Co. Ltd. Metropolitan Vickers were successors to British Westinghouse.

Acknowledgments and Sources

This book is based on Chapter 6 of *Great British Tramway Networks* by W. H. Bett and J C. Gillham (Fourth Edition. LRTL 1962) with additional information from recent books and articles as listed in the bibliography.

The original fleet lists were compiled by the late J. H. Price with the valued assistance of G.H.F. Atkins, R. Brook, T. Barker, A.W.Brotchie, R. Elliott, J.C. Gillham, F.P.Groves, R. Marshall, M.J. O'Connor, A.J.Pitman, H.B. Priestley and R.G.P. Tebb. The Mansfield fleet list has been corrected by Tony Hurst, the Crich and Nottingham Express Transit lists were compiled by R.J.S. Wiseman with help from Glynn Wilton and Clive Pennington.

The maps have been drawn by R.A.Smith for Chesterfield. Ashover, Crich, Burton and Ashby and Lincoln, also the area map based on an original by J.C.Gillham. Those for Derby, Burton-on-Trent, Mansfield, Nottingham and Leicester are based on those by J.C. Gillham. That for Matlock is based on the Ordnance Survey, courtesy Matlock Library

The cover is from a painting by Ashley Best, The photographs including those by W.A.Camwell, C. Lane, Dr H Nicol, M. J. O'Connor, H.B.Priestley and S.L. Smith have been have been reproduced by courtesy of the Tramway Museum Society with special thanks to Glynn Wilton and Chris Gent.

Thanks are due to Derbyshire Library Service for the valuable assistance provided by Matlock Library, and to G. B. Claydon, who kindly read the text and made suggestions for its improvement.

Trent Bridge Tram terminus, Nottingham.   *(Commercial Card*

Bibliography - General

Great British Tramway Networks.
    by W.H. Bett and J.C.Gillham.(Light Railway Transport League, 4th Edition 1972)
What Colour Was That Tram ?
    by David Voice (Author, 4th Edition, 1998)
The Definitive Guide to Trams (including funiculars) in the British Isles
    by David Voice (Adam Gordon, 2001).

Alford & Sutton Tramway
Alford & Sutton Tramway,
        by George Dow (Author, 1984)
A Regional History of the Railways of Great Britain, Volume 9, East Midlands,
        by Robin Leleux, (David & Charles, 1976)

Ashover Light Railway
The Ashover Light Railway,
        by K.P.Plant (Oakwood Press, 1965)
A Regional History of the Railways of Great Britain, Volume 9, East Midlands,
        by Robin Leleux, (David & Charles, 1976
Forgotten Railways: Volume 2, The East Midlands,
        by P. Howard Anderson (Revised edition, David St. John Thomas, 1985)

Burton on Trent
An English Country Tramway,
        by R.B. Parr (National Tramway Museum, 1970)
Burton & Ashby Tramways,
        by Peter M. White (Middleton Press, 2000)
Also an unpublished history of Burton Corporation Tramways by R. Marshall

Chesterfield
Chesterfield Tramways,
        by C.C.Hall   (in *Tramway Review* Nos. 65-67, 69, 1971)
Chesterfield Tramways,
        by Barry Marsden (Middleton Press, 2004)

Crich Tramway Village
Tramway Adventure
        by Ian Yearsley (National Tramway Museum, 1998)
The National Tramway Museum (Illustrated Guide Book)
Tramway Museum Stock Book,
        by Ian Stewart (Dianswell Publications, 1992)

Derby
Derby Tramways
        by Colin Barker (Middleton Press, 2003)
Derby Corporation Tramways.
        by M.J. O'Connor.(in *Modern Tramway* Nos. 133-4, 1949)

Leicester

Leicester's Trams in Retrospect,
   by M.S.W.Pearson.(National Tramway Museum 1970)
Tramways in Leicester
   by M.S.W.Pearson.(National Tramway Museum 1988)
Leicester's Trams,
   by Geoff Creese . (Irwell Press, 2000)

Lincoln

The Tramways of the City of Lincoln,
   by D.H. Yarnell (In *Tramway Review* Nos. 63-65)

Loughborough

The Brush Electrical Engineering Company Ltd. & Its Tramcars
   by J.H.Price (Tramway & Light Rail Society, 1976)

Mansfield

Mansfield's Trams,
   by Tony Hurst. (Irwell Press, 2002)

Matlock

The Matlock Cable Tramway,
   by C.C.Hall (in *Tramway Review* No 5, 1951)

Nottingham

A History of Nottingham City Transport, 1897 - 1959
   (by R. Marshall. Nottingham City Transport, 1960)
The Horse Tramways in Nottingham,
   by R.B. Parr.(in *Tramway Review* No 2, 1950)
Nottingham City Transport,
   by F.P. Groves.(Transport Publishing Company, 1978)
Trent Bridge to Bulwell by Tram,
   by R.J.S.Wiseman.(in *Tramway Review* No 197, 2004)

Nottinghamshire

The Nottinghamshire & Derbyshire Tramway,
   by M.J. O'Connor (in *Trams* No.24, Tramway Museum Society, 1967)
Nottinghamshire & Derbyshire Tramways,
   by L. Marston.(in *Tramway Review* No 126, 127, 1986)

Skegness

Skeggy - The Story of an East Coast Town
   by William Kime.(Seashell Books, 1971)

Trams at Skegness (note in Tramway Review Nos. 138, 1989)

A quiet day as Derby Corporation No. 30 passes a horse and cart on the tree-lined Osmaston Road.
(Commercial card

No.68 on Service 2 to Narborough Road has turned the corner from East Park Road into Evington Road
n 7 May 1938. *(W.A. Camwell, courtesy National Tramway Museum*

Light Rail Transit Association

Advocating modern tramways and urban light rail transit

The Light Rail Transit Association is an international organisation dedicated to campaigning for better fixed-track public transport, in particular tramways (usually on-street) and light rail (usually off-street but very accessible).

Membership of the LRTA is open equally to professional organisations, transport planners and individuals with a particular interest in the subject. Members receive free of charge by post Tramways & Urban Transit, the all-colour monthly A4-size magazine, as part of their subscription. With tramway and light rail systems being adopted not only in Europe but world-wide, this high-quality journal features topical articles and extensive news coverage, also trade news, book reviews and readers' letters. Details of local meetings in the British Isles are included.

LRTA Officers (many with transport industry experience) have extensive knowledge of light rail and tramway applications, and a library of all our publications, campaigning and historical, is maintained.

LRTA Subscriptions & Membership information:
38 Wolseley Road, Sale, Greater Manchester M33 7AU
membership@lrta.org

General LRTA Enquiries:
24 Northdowns, Cranleigh, Surrey GU6 8BX
secretary@lrta.org

LRTA Publications:
14 Prae Close, St. Albans, Herts. AL3 4SF
publications@lrta.org)

FOR FURTHER INFORMATION
VISIT THE LRTA WEBSITE: www.lrta.org

Back Cover
The Incentro trams of Nottingham Express Transit run in all weather conditions. In the upper view No 20 is seen ascending from the Forest stop up snow covered Mount Hooton Road o while below a car descend Waverley Street on a wet afternoon overshadowed by the trees of the arboretum. 15 October 2004.
(R.J.S.Wisema